WHY TOMMY ISN'T LEARNING

On the following two pages we reproduce two exam papers: one an 11+ maths paper, 1924, the other a Teachers Training College maths grading test for eighteen- or nineteen-year-olds in the 1960s.

S. H. Frome discusses the implications of these two test papers in Chapter 4.

1. A centimetre of wire weighs 0·93 gramme. What is the length (to the nearest centimetre) of a piece weighing 100 grammes?

2. A bicycle wheel travels 7 feet 4 inches for each revolution of the back wheel. If the wheel revolves twice in every second, at what rate in miles per hour is the bicycle travelling?

3. On a map on the scale of 6 inches to the mile, a rectangular field appears as 1·7 inches long and 0·8 inch broad. Find in yards the length of fencing required to enclose it; and find its area in acres.

4. Divide 0·37044 by 0·0147

5. Simplify: $\dfrac{2\frac{1}{5} - \frac{1}{2} \text{ of } 3\frac{1}{3}}{3 + 1\frac{2}{5}}$

6. A man cycling at 10 miles per hour passes a man walking at 4 miles per hour. Twelve minutes later the bicyclist has a puncture. How far ahead of the walker is he when this happens? If the cyclist takes 20 minutes to mend the puncture, will the man walking pass him while he is mending it or not? How far apart will the two men be when the bicyclist is ready to start again?

7. What is the difference in decimetres between: (a) 4 metres, 3 centimetres, 5 millimetres, and (b) 2 metres, 1 decimetre, 8 centimetres?

8. Seven collecting boxes contained respectively £2. 3s. 6½d.; 18s. 9d.; £1. 0s. 11d.; 4s. 0¾d.; £1. 3s. 8d.; 19s. 5d.; and 2s. 7d.

Find:

    (a) The total amount of all sums above £1.
    (b) The total amount of all sums under £1.
    (c) Whether the largest amount was greater or smaller than the sum of the three smallest amounts and by how much.

RECENT MATHEMATICS GRADING TEST—
TEACHERS TRAINING COLLEGE

1. $6{,}453 + 7{,}483 + 7{,}962 + 5{,}948$

2. $7{,}009 - 5{,}436$

3. A car running 22 miles to the gallon of petrol uses 14 gallons for a certain journey. How many gallons would be used for the same journey by a car which runs 28 miles to the gallon?

4. $4 \cdot 56 \div 0 \cdot 19$

5. $2\frac{1}{3} + \frac{5}{12} - 1\frac{7}{8}$

6. A train travelling at an average speed of 39 m.p.h. can do a certain journey in 4 hours. How long would the same journey take at an average speed of 52 m.p.h.?

7. In a roll of print material there were 40 yd. Nine girls made themselves dresses, each taking $3\frac{1}{2}$ yd. of material. How much print was left in the roll?

8. How much change would there be from £1 after paying for $3\frac{1}{2}$ lb. at 1s. 9d. per lb.?

Stuart Froome has established a reputation as Headmaster of a primary school run on sound practical lines. He began his teaching career as a student teacher at seventeen. This experience, he says, was invaluable in learning how to control very large classes —an almost universal problem, even today. After training at St. Luke's College, Exeter, he began teaching in Surrey and has remained there ever since. He has been a headmaster for nearly thirty years: fourteen in a full-range school (seven to fifteen years), and sixteen in his present post, St. Jude's Junior School at Englefield Green.

He is a past President of Thames Valley National Union of Teachers Association, and was the first President of the North-West Surrey Association of Head Teachers. Mr. Froome is deeply involved in the young generation, not only as the headmaster of the small children whose educational fate he is writing about in *Why Tommy Isn't Learning* but also at the level of further education. He has been the Principal of a large evening institute in Egham for many years, and was the first Honorary Secretary of the Egham Youth Council.

As a writer, Mr. Froome came to prominence as a contributor to the *Sunday Express* and to the well-known *Black Paper* on education published during 1969. A consistent pleader of the cause of common sense in education—amid growing public alarm at the decline in standards that fashionable notions in teaching have brought about—he has seized the opportunity in his book *Why Tommy Isn't Learning* to give parents and teachers throughout Britain their first full warning of what is happening in the school life of the children who are the object of their responsibility and love.

ABOUT THIS BOOK

The chances are it's not that Tommy's too slow or too idle—it's that he isn't being taught properly. Mr. Froome addresses himself to the millions of parents whose children are being handicapped by present-day fashionable teaching methods. He shows clearly that the standard of achievement by children in all the basic subjects, both in ability and in knowledge, has fallen appreciably over the last forty years.

Long experience and an independent mind have left him convinced that 'learning by stealth' does not and cannot work with the great majority of children. What children need is simple, affectionate discipline, set rules and a definite direction, if they are to develop their minds, personalities and talents to the full. Growing numbers of parents throughout Britain have long suspected that this is true—but have felt helpless to do anything about it. At the same time, Mr. Froome points out, in detail, how the standards of teacher training have declined and what the effect has been on pupils.

Mr. Froome knows that there are thousands of teachers in Britain doing a conscientious job, working overtime for very little pay, teachers who love children and are proud of their profession. They are tired of being criticised and carped at—especially by parents who drop in to say that Tommy isn't learning as he should. To these teachers Mr. Froome simply says: *It is not your fault—you have been misled for years by educators who do not know the classroom or children as well as you do.*

WHY TOMMY
ISN'T LEARNING

S. H. FROOME

TOM STACEY LTD

Tom Stacey Ltd, 11a Stratford Road,
London W.8. England

First published 1970

Copyright © S. H. Froome

SBN 85468 012 8

Printed in Great Britain by
Richard Clay (The Chaucer Press), Ltd.,
Bungay, Suffolk

CONTENTS

ACKNOWLEDGEMENTS

I am grateful to Professor G. H. Bantock for allowing me to quote from his essay 'Discovery Methods', and to Professor Sir Cyril Burt for his kind permission to quote from his articles in the *Journal of the Association of Educational Psychologists* and in *Black Paper Two*; to Professor Brian Cox for allowing me to use material from my articles in the *Critical Survey* and the second *Black Paper*; to Ronald Deadman, Editor of *Teachers World*, for similar use of articles; to Keith Gardner for leave to quote from *Crisis in the Classroom*; to Maurice Harrison, former Director of Education for Oldham, for letting me quote from his book, *Teaching Reading—an i.t.a. Approach*; to Mrs. Betty Root for allowing me to quote her views on reading retardation, and finally to Mr. A. Almond for much very helpful advice.

'IT DON'T WORK!'
A GENERAL COMMENT

Towards the end of the summer term is a busy time in
most schools. Tests of various kinds have to be set and
marked, and pupils have to be allocated to the classes
they will be working in during the next educational year.
In many schools reports on children have to be sent
out to parents, and these involve all members of staff in
additional work. This period of examinations and reports is, of course, an anxious time for parents, and
many of them request interviews with the headteacher to discuss the progress of their children. Not
all, by any means, are satisfied with the way their offspring have 'got on', and often there is open criticism
of what are called 'modern methods' of teaching, and
something referred to as 'The Playway', which is held
responsible for an alleged lowering of standards in the
schools.

One interview I had with an anxious parent concerned her son's poor reading ability, which at the age
of nine was equivalent to that of a child of seven when
measured on a standard reading test. This mother could
not understand why her son could not read as well as
his sister had done at the same age, because in her
opinion he was just as intelligent, and it certainly had
to be admitted that in looks and physical development
he was very similar to his 'superior' sister. She was
obviously very disappointed and even ashamed of her
boy's backwardness in reading, and she told a story

about it which brought home to me how large such matters loom in the average parent's life.

Two years previously, when Tommy was seven and could barely read half a dozen words, his family had gone on holiday to Cornwall. One day while motoring in a lonely coastal district they had pulled up at a one-pump filling-station, only to find a cardboard notice on the pump which read, 'Out of Order.' As the car was running short of fuel, father called at the house near by to seek assistance, and mother and the two children were left in the car. Margaret, the sister, explained to her little brother quite helpfully, albeit perhaps in a patronising manner, that they would have to get their petrol somewhere else. 'I know,' replied Tommy, 'it says so on the pump.' 'How do you know?' retorted Margaret, 'you can't read!' 'Yes I can,' claimed her brother, boldly trying to keep his end up. 'Go on then, read it!' challenged Margaret, and Tommy, making a last, feeble bid to hold his own, looked hard at the notice on the pump and said, 'It don't work.' Margaret and Dad hooted with laughter at this exposure of Tommy's weakness, but Mother told me sadly, 'I didn't laugh; I nearly cried with shame for the boy, because I wondered what was to become of him if he didn't learn to read.'

Not long ago a father of a boy of eight in the first year came to see me about another matter. His clever little boy was a fluent reader, (he had already read *Treasure Island*), but father, who was studying as a mature student at a nearby teachers' training college, was worried about his son's spelling. 'I want John to be a good speller,' he said, 'because I have seen how embarrassing it is for so many of the younger students at college, many of whom are shocking spellers and are

ashamed of it.' He then showed me a copy of a dupli-
cated letter which he had received from the chairman
of the Summer Fête Committee of a London University
college department inviting local people to attend the
summer fête in aid of Cancer Research. This letter,
presumably written by a university undergraduate,
contained the following sentences: 'We are holding
displays of judo, fencing and folk-dancing; fashion and
tallent shows; childrens games and fancy dress. I hope
you and your family will take the oportunity of visiting
the college and seeing the wide range of tallents of the
students.' As this parent said, 'Obviously spelling and
punctuation will not be two of the talents on show at
this fête, if the chairman's letter is any indication of the
standards achieved.' I was bound to agree with him,
and then tried to reassure him about his boy's alleged
weakness in spelling, which I thought would improve
when he was given word lists to learn systematically.

Both of these parents were worried about their
children's standards of achievement at school, but they
were making the understandable mistake of supposing
that children of today would be at least as capable in
reading and spelling as they themselves were at the
same age. They were, in fact, judging their children's
progress at school on what they remembered of their
own education thirty or forty years ago, and they had
not taken into account that in the past three or four
decades there has been an appreciable decline in the
standards of reading, writing and arithmetic in state
schools.

Now this may seem a surprising statement when it is
considered that the cost of education in this country has
soared so much since the last war that it is now higher
than that of defence, but anyone who has read

Professor Parkinson on the subject of business efficiency will know that increased costs and appointment of more personnel do not necessarily bring about increased productivity. Certainly there are more teachers employed in this country than ever before, and classes have diminished in size correspondingly, but there has not been the expected improvement in standards of achievement in the basic subjects of the curriculum. On the contrary, there are definite signs of a decline in standards.

Evidence for this assertion is not based on the two incidents related above, although these are, of course, indicative of parents' concern about the quality of modern schooling. University undergraduates unable to spell words like 'talents' and 'opportunity' are nowadays not by any means uncommon, and backward readers like nine-year-old Tommy are certainly not diminishing in number.

How has this situation come about? How is it that one hundred years after Mr. Forster's Education Act of 1870 provided state education for the poorest section of the community, and paved the way for a literate population, standards of literacy seem to be deteriorating for the population as a whole? It would have been reasonable to suppose that after the effects of compulsory education for all had been felt, and one complete generation had been taught to read, to write and to calculate, the descendants of these people would have become progressively better educated as generation succeeded generation. There is no doubt that immediately after the passing of the Forster Act, when the working classes had become used to having to send their children to school, there was a tremendous enthusiasm for education in this country, and the poor began to realise the immense advantages to be gained by having their sons and daughters taught the elements of the basic subjects of the school curriculum. Reading, writing and arithmetic were valued as the keys to learning, and in those days there was only one recognised method of imparting to children a sound knowledge of those subjects.

Put simply, this method was based on the authority of the teacher, whose task it was to present to the pupils lessons from a clearly defined syllabus of instruction, in as interesting a manner as possible, and to ensure that the most important facts in those lessons were remembered, making, of course, due allowance for the differing mental capacities of the children. The teacher used the time-honoured didactic method, because the sensible assumption was made that, being an educated adult himself, he had a valuable store of information to impart to the untutored children in his care. Classes in those days of the early elementary system were usually fifty or sixty in number and, because of poor accommodation, there would often be over one hundred children in the same room at the same time, with teachers and monitors coping with widely differing age groups simultaneously. Under such conditions the teacher's power of class control was the most important quality to be considered. Without this power he or she was helpless, and so in those times no higher recommendation could be given to a teacher than to be regarded as a sound disciplinarian. It was a tough system, and only strong teachers survived, but as far as inculcation of the basic subjects of the curriculum went, it was most efficient. At the turn of the century, and for the first twenty years of this one, most children left school well grounded in reading, writing and arithmetic, and for good measure they also had a sound knowledge of history, geography, nature study and scripture. They had also been taught to sing and to do physical exercises, and for practical work the girls had been instructed in needlework and the boys in woodwork. Above all however, they had learnt through firm discipline the value of effort and concentration in acquiring the basic skills necessary for a fuller education.

There were no doubt faults in the early elementary system of education. Size of classes, poor accommodation and shortage of materials dictated a rigidity of method and a conformity of outlook which in these days would not be considered desirable, but the efficiency of the system cannot be contested. The great majority of the children were turned out into the world at fourteen years of age able to write a simple letter with correct spelling, punctuation and grammatical construction; they were good readers, and they were reasonably accurate in dealing with the British system of money, weights and measures. Moreover, the clever ones could, through scholarship awards, pass on to secondary schools and the university.

It would have been understandable that with such an efficient elementary system of education the didactic method and the philosophy upon which it was based would have continued with little modification other than efforts to diminish the size of classes. However, this is not the case. Far from the system being preserved, it has been under attack from many quarters over the past three or four decades. Discipline and order in schools, instead of being regarded as desirable ends, are criticised as repressive influences; children working peacefully in rows of desks are said to be 'slavishly sitting in serried ranks', while the quiet and tranquillity which were formerly the hall-marks of the classroom of the successful teacher are now qualities to be sneered at. This quotation from the handbook of a London training college issued to students when about to begin school practice sums up the modern attitude to teaching: 'Absolute silence in the classroom used to be regarded as a sign of health; it is now regarded as a sign of death.' Students could receive no clearer indication that if they wish to be thought up-to-date and progressive, then they must at all costs encourage their classes to make a din. Noise, it would appear, is synonymous with healthy activity.

It has been the promulgation of this new doctrine of activity methods which has in my opinion caused a deterioration in standards of achievement in the basic subjects of the curriculum, and with it a falling-off in children's effort and attitude to work which is a poor preparation for the business of living. Teachers themselves are bemused by the many fashionable new trends which they are encouraged to follow, and many of the older ones are dismayed at the neglect of the tried and tested methods of learning which used to provide the basic structure of knowledge and intellectual skills on which children could build for the rest of their education and their life.

I shall try in this book to adduce evidence concerning falling standards in the basic subjects, and shall endeavour to show how the easy acceptance of a new philosophy and method of learning was responsible for this sad deterioration. I shall hope, too, to make some suggestions for halting the decline in educational standards before it is too late.

2

TAKING TOO LONG TO READ

I have been in teaching for over forty years, and during that time I have gained a general impression that standards of reading, writing and arithmetic have been steadily deteriorating. By this I mean that there has been a slowing down of learning so that the standard of achievement reached by a child in school today is anything up to a year behind that of a child of thirty or forty years ago. This retardation of learning is not surprising, because with the new concept of a 'child-centred' education the pace of progress is left to the child, and he is never pressed to pursue a particular path of subject study. He must not be inculcated with facts by what is derisively referred to as 'parrot-like repetition', but by purely spontaneous motivation he must discover for himself all that he needs to know. This grand, libertarian theory of education is in my view more than anything else responsible for the decline in scholarship which I maintain has taken place.

It is in reading ability that children in the infant (up to seven) and junior (up to eleven) departments of schools show such a retardation compared with those of the thirties. In 1931, the Board of Education's Consultative Committee on the Primary School suggested that the task of the junior school teacher was mainly that of developing reading comprehension, since only a few 'backward' children would be in need of systematic instruction in reading mechanics after the age of seven. Such a statement today would bring wry smiles of incredulity from the teachers who have to take the newly entered seven-year-olds in the junior schools. Far from being able to concentrate on the comprehension side of reading, the junior schools have to put all their energies into teaching many of the newly admitted first-year children the basic sounds of the letters of the alphabet, because the prevailing fashion of teaching by the 'look and say' method has not equipped them with a phonetic basis of reading. In case this may be considered an exaggeration, let me quote from a recent publication, *Reading in Infant Classes* by Dr. E. J. Goodacre, 1967. This report under the auspices of the National Foundation for Educational Research was based on an enquiry into teaching practice and conditions in 100 schools in the County of Kent. This area is one where the majority of the children come from homes which are termed of 'high socio-economic status', and yet this report says. 'One of the findings of the Kent enquiry was that although pupils' standards of achievement at seven years of age varied from school to school and area to area, about 45 per cent of the children still needed the kind of teaching associated with the infant school at the time of their transfer to the junior school.' So much for the assumptions of the Consultative Committee in 1931!

Standards in the 'bad old days' at the turn of the century were very different. In the school in which I now work, the headmaster of that period was accustomed to test his infant intake by asking them to read from the first reader of the junior school, and those who could not (a mere odd one or two) were sent back to the infant school until they were ready. Such a practice would not be possible in these days, because the numbers would be too great for many infants' schools to retain.

The decline in reading standards was, after 1945, usually attributed to the war, and of course the effects of evacuation and bombing must carry some of the responsibility. There was in fact at this time great concern in the country generally about the large increase in backward readers, so that a number of local authorities conducted reading surveys in their areas in an effort to find the extent of the alleged reading retardation. Brighton, Burton-upon-Trent, Middlesbrough, Leeds, Swansea and Monmouthshire are some of the localities where these investigations took place. In Dr. Joyce Morris's book, *Reading in the Primary School*, the results of these surveys are summarised and we are told that in Brighton in 1947 the whole school population between the ages of six years six months and eleven years eleven months was tested by means of Burt's Reading Accuracy Test.[1] A retarded child, for the purpose of the test, was one whose standard of work was below that achieved by average children 20 per cent younger than himself. Before the war it was estimated that about 10 per cent of the total school population, aged ten to eleven, could be classified as being retarded on this basis. The Brighton report revealed that the actual number of the children tested who were classified as seriously retarded, using the pre-war criterion, was considerably higher than the number before 1939. In one school as many as 64 per cent of children were more than a year retarded, while in other schools the figures were 16, 20, 21 and 22 per cent. It was later pointed out by the Ministry in 1950 that if Professor Vernon's (1938) norms[2] had been used instead

---

[1] A standardised Reading Test devised by the British psychologist, Professor Sir Cyril Burt, and commonly used in Great Britain.

[2] Norms are standards derived from the results of previous tests.

of those produced by Burt in 1921, then as many as 32 per cent of children in their last year of primary schooling must be regarded as retarded readers. It should be noted here that before the war a child was considered retarded if his reading quotient was below 85 (average attainment 100), not the lower figure of 80 used subsequently.

When it is considered that Brighton is, like Kent, an area of 'high socio-economic status' this figure of 32 per cent retarded readers was surprisingly high, and clearly in the slum areas of big industrial cities the position could well have been much worse.

The Burton-upon-Trent survey taken in 1947 used different tests, but the results followed the same pattern as Brighton's. Approximately 23 per cent of the tested children had reading ages two years or more below their mental ages. Moreover, after the eleven-plus children had gone to their grammar schools, among the two-thirds who went to the secondary modern schools no less than 40 per cent were retarded by two years or more. What a problem these children must have been in their reception schools!

The surveys held in Middlesbrough and Leeds in 1953, and in Swansea and Monmouthshire in 1954, revealed that these areas also were not without the problem of an increased proportion of backward readers who needed special attention in school.

The results of these local surveys of reading standards were alarming, and if they could be taken as indicative of what was happening in the country generally, then the Consultative Committee's 1931 forecast that there would soon be only a few children at seven in need of systematic instruction in the mechanics of reading would have been proved to be only a pipe-dream. In

1948, the Ministry of Education determined to make a survey of its own on a national scale, and compare the national norms for two age-groups with corresponding pre-war ones. The findings of this survey merely confirmed the shocking decline revealed by the six local investigations. There were approximately 30 per cent of fifteen-year-olds and 23 per cent of eleven-year-olds who were classified as 'backward readers' as against the pre-war 10 per cent. Moreover, a general lowering of reading standards was admitted in this statement: 'The ability to read of pupils of eleven years and fifteen years old was found on the average to be behind that of their pre-war counterparts by 12 months and 22 months respectively.'

The publishing of these findings had one good effect. It shocked the public, and it shook educationists generally out of their complacent notions that a general improvement in scholastic standards was a continuously inevitable process. Immediately after the reports, local education authorities and the Ministry made strenuous efforts to improve reading standards by encouraging remedial centres to be set up, and schools were urged to have special backward groups taken by experienced members of staff. In addition, numerous courses in the teaching of backward readers were arranged in an effort to obliterate the stigma of reading backwardness which sullied the good name of English education. Surveys conducted since 1948 have certainly shown progressive improvement in national standards of reading, but the advances made are not as good as they appear. For instance, the one in 1956 claimed that the age group born in 1945 were in 1956 on average nine months more advanced than their predecessors born in 1937 were in 1948. This improvement is not as good as it sounds when one notices that the 1937 baby was only two when war broke out, and was learning to read under the worst conditions of this century. As Keith Gardner points out in the book *Crisis in the Classroom*, 'At first sight these reading surveys have produced satisfactory results. In 1964, our fifteen-year-old pupils were two years advanced over similar pupils in 1948. This looks like progress. However, a disturbing analysis by Professor Vernon of London has been completely ignored. This revealed that in 1948, which was taken as the base-line for subsequent reports, reading standards were at a very low ebb. Education had suffered from the war years and children in 1948 were $1\frac{1}{2}$ years below the standard in 1939. So what has been hailed as magnificent progress since the Second World War has, in fact, barely repaired the damage sustained in our fight for survival. This in spite of the 1944 Education Act, the massive re-building of schools, the extension of teacher training, and the increase in interest in education.'

If evidence is needed that reading standards in school today are not satisfactory, we have only to turn to the recently expressed view of Mrs. Betty Root, who is the Tutor/Organiser of the Centre for the Teaching of Reading at the Institute of Education, Reading University. Mrs. Root, a trained qualified teacher, is an expert in the teaching of reading and knows the difficulties of the subject from first-hand experience in schools. In this respect she is unlike so many of the pundits who offer advice on the problems of education but have had little experience of actual teaching the pupils about whom they appear so knowledgeable. At Mrs. Root's reading centre, which is the only one of its kind in the country, all the reading courses in use in

England and America are on show, and the tutor is there to advise and help on the use of them. There are no less than thirty-four different systems available, many of which have various mechanical aids which need explanation to the layman. Despite the large number of teaching methods from which teachers can choose, Mrs. Root claims that there are more backward readers in the country than ever. She further states that lack of available statistics before 1945 makes comparisons difficult, but it is clear from the post-war pattern that children, through no fault of their own, are not learning to read in the early stages as they used to. Reading, she maintains, is a fairly complex subject, and it is now clear that children '*do not just pick it up as they go along*'.

Those last eight italicised words are symptomatic of the new ideas which are affecting all aspects of English education. For many years now educational experts have been advising teachers not to make things too difficult for children and not to press them on at too fast a pace. 'They will read when they are ready,' we are told, 'if they are not harassed into premature contact with things which are too difficult for them.' In other words, we must let them learn to read in their own way and in their own good time.

If this 'picking it up as you go along' theory is the basis of our educational thinking today there would not appear to be much point in parents sending their children to school. Keith Gardner, whom I quoted above, has written, 'In the post-war infant school it has been considered slightly old-fashioned to teach reading at all. In the modern craze for child-centred education, *reading has become something that is acquired—not taught.*' From 1961 to 1967 he studied trends in early reading standards in the junior schools of one area. From the results of this investigation, he estimated that in 1961 25 per cent of 2,000 first-year primary school pupils had not made a start in learning to read. In every subsequent year of this study he found the number had increased, until by 1967 it had reached the astounding figure of 40 per cent. It would appear that if this trend continues and children are expected to begin reading only when they are ready, then the process of learning to read will suffer progressive postponement until the whole vital mechanics of the operation will be conducted in the junior school. This state of affairs will doubtless please the proponents of the playway system, but parents will, I think, do as in Russia and teach their children to read at home.

In the Soviet Union children start school during their seventh year and are expected to be able to read before this great day arrives. There is much propaganda urging people to teach their offspring to read at five, and posters showing aunts, uncles and other relations helping in this process are on show in public places. It seems to work, and the vast majority of children enter school able to begin serious reading in all subjects of the curriculum. Russia cannot afford to squander money or manpower, and by cutting out the two to three years which English children spend in the jolly play atmosphere of our infants' schools, more money is available for the deadly serious business of learning after seven.

Corroboration of the decline in reading standards which I have shown above is provided by a comparison of the reading books of today with those in use in schools forty years ago. Publishers have had to come to terms with the modern tendency to postpone reading until the child is 'ready', and so the kind of reading matter which in vocabulary and literary style was considered suitable for a child in 1920 would today have to be offered to children two or three years older. Many boys' and girls' classics have now to be presented in abridged form, and to retain the size of the volume, print becomes bigger and the pictures more numerous. In a typical class reader published by Collins and in use in schools at the turn of the century, Standard Five children, aged eleven, were expected to read extracts from learned articles in *The Times* and *Saturday Magazine* on such subjects as Migration of Labour, The Trade Winds, A Carlist Faction Chief and The Overflow of the Nile. These extracts, couched in typical *Times* prose, together with pieces from Macaulay's *Essays*, and for light relief two from Addison's *Sir Roger de Coverley*, were interspersed with poems by Wordsworth, Scott, Gray, Southey and Goldsmith. A child of eleven in these days, nurtured on a diet of Enid Blyton and Hergé's *Adventures of Tin-Tin*, would find such reading matter beyond him, and yet we must suppose that such difficult passages were the customary fare of average children when this book was produced. It was, of course, a feature of education in those days that all learning was based on reading; and in geography, history, scripture and nature study, after the formal lesson had been given by the teacher, it was usual to supplement the information received by more gleaned from a subject reader. Reading around the class from history and geography readers was usual until after the last war, and this practice in reading aloud under the critical ear of both the teacher and classmates was a tremendous incentive to clear enunciation and to appreciation of the uses of punctuation. Today, reading around the class is out, and class readers in history and geography are therefore few in number and much attenuated in reading content. Visual or pictorial readers with one page of letterpress facing a page of drawings and diagrams are today the vogue. Perhaps one day the comic-strip will provide all the reading considered necessary for the watered-down history and geography which come under that rather loose term 'Social Studies'.

Lest it may be thought that I have exaggerated the deficiencies of the reading situation in the schools and their effect on the young people who leave for industry or further education, let me quote from some recent research made into the reading standards of students admitted into technical colleges. In the book *Teaching Reading—an I.T.A. Approach* by Mr. M. Harrison, the former Director of Education for Oldham, it says, 'Dr. J. Gardner, Head of the Department of Humanities at Bradford Technical College, reporting recently on research into the reading ability of some 800 students in two well-known technical colleges, says that 55% find "actual mechanical problems in reading sufficient to ensure that they do not have great success in any examination which includes the understanding of written work". 22% had such problems that they were unlikely to have any success in written examinations, and 28% exhibited ignorance of a [normal] thirteen-year-old's vocabulary.' Dr. Gardner writes, 'In order to succeed in City and Guilds courses it is virtually essential to have a fourteen-year-old vocabulary attainment. It is thus quite clear that the odds are weighted from the beginning against a substantial minority of those students who attempt the courses. The work is too hard for them in basic communication.' So much for the reading skill of technical-college students in this brave new technological age!

I think I have said enough to show that all is far from right with the standard of reading in the schools of this country. I shall try to show in Chapter 8 what I think are the root causes of the decline in achievement, and suggest how the situation might be improved.

3

THE DECLINE IN WRITTEN ENGLISH

Whenever the English master at my grammar school came across a particularly vile piece of spoken or written work, he would say to the boy who had perpetrated it, 'Bestest Inglish Spikked Hear', which words he maintained he had once seen on a notice in a French *estaminet* in the First World War. This phrase became a little overworked as time went on, but it was always good for a laugh, and we were careful to avoid the kind of mistakes in language which earned this form of rebuke. I was reminded of this a few years ago when I was taking the first lesson of the session with a class of G.C.E. English evening-school students. They were a mixed bag, and in order to get some idea of their capabilities I dictated to them a passage from one of Leigh Hunt's essays. We swapped books and marked it on the spot, and to the chagrin of the young English people who made up the bulk of the class, and to the obvious embarrassment of the *fraulein*, we found that the only student with no mistakes was a German *au pair* girl who had been in the country for only two years. I was not surprised at this, because I knew how spelling has been neglected in this country for the past thirty or forty years, but I was not a little ashamed to have to admit that the 'Bestest Inglish' had been written by a foreigner.

When I first began to teach, dictation was recognised as one of the most effective aids to accurate written English. Most school classes had a daily dictation period, and dictation was used in many public examinations as a reliable indicator or the candidates' mastery of the language. The identity of the expert advisers who between the two great wars gradually persuaded teachers to drop dictation from the time-table has not come to light; but in the *Handbook of Suggestions for Teachers* issued by the Board of Education in 1937 there was almost a directive against using this time-tested method of teaching children to write accurately. This is what was said, 'As a regular and definite constituent of the teaching of English, dictation is to be deprecated. It is a convenient method of testing spellings that have already been committed to memory, although it is of no value in the direct teaching of spelling.' There is no doubt that the following of the advice given in those two sentences is largely responsible for the sorry state of English spelling, which at present mars much of the written work in our schools.

Poor spelling is found at all levels of education today. It starts in the primary and junior schools, where the attempts to teach reading without a phonetic basis not only retard achievement by one or two years, but also through the partial neglect of letter-sounds give the child no sound grounding on which to develop his spelling powers. Moreover, the inability of the child to break up polysyllabic words into bits which can be sounded is one of the disadvantages of the 'look and say' or 'whole word' method of teaching reading. Many common spelling errors could be avoided if children knew how to transpose into letters the sounds which syllables make. The undergraduate whom I quoted as not being able to spell 'talents' and 'opportunity' would not, I think, have put one too many 'l's' in the former and one too few 'p's' in the latter if she had been more aware of the sounds of 'tall' and 'open'. Similarly, the young teacher whom I recently requested to rewrite two school reports because she had put 'consistant' and 'occassionally' in them, clearly was not very conscious of the 'ant' and 'ass' sounds in the words, but was writing them from vaguely remembered shapes.

The bad spelling in the junior schools is carried on to the secondaries, where the modern inspectorial advice not to bother about it but to concentrate on free creative writing, leads to the sorry situation we have today when teachers' training college entrants have to be taught to spell by their tutors. In case this may be regarded as overstatement, I give below a copy of an aid to spelling provided to first-year entrants to a large training college which has a good reputation and where the more able students can study for their B.Ed..

'SPELLING'

'Below is a list of 100 words. The average college man who learns to spell all these should nearly halve his spelling mistakes. The words are arranged in two groups of 50, the first group being particularly important. The number after each word is the percentage that misspelt it in a sample of first and second year men. On the other side of this sheet are five spelling tips.'

From the two lists of 50 given words I have selected twenty-five which are everyday words and which one would have been expected to spell correctly at the age of twelve in the 'bad old days' of spelling lists and dictation. The percentages of training college students unable to spell them should be a timely warning to observers of the educational scene. They show how standards have deteriorated in the schools since the adoption of the 'writing-without-restraint' theory has dominated the teaching of English.

*Percentage of misspellings in college sample of first and
second year men*

accommodation	60	conscientious	64
acquaintance	53	principal	44
all right	70	disastrous	49
benefiting	53	foresee	46
appalling	53	humorous	58
conscious	53	lightning	48
embarrass	54	remembrance	50
exaggerate	61	rhythm	50
fulfil	53	supersede	83
manoeuvre	85	deterrent	43
occurrence	71	possess	40
privilege	59	practise	38
transferred	40		

One can only feel sympathy for the college lecturers
in English and other subjects where written work is
expected, at the clear evidence of student incompetence
in spelling which the above list reveals. How did these
young men of eighteen and over get into a training
college? How low is the standard of G.C.E. English
which allows people of this calibre to claim they have
the necessary 'O' level certificate in this most important
subject and so gain admission to teaching? How can
the 50 per cent of men who could not spell 'rhythm'
honestly take English and English Literature with
classes of schoolchildren? Finally, what can be the
effect on children when they are taught by teachers who
are so clearly lacking in the rudiments of their language?

The lecturers at this college should be commended
for not shutting their eyes to student shortcomings, and
for making some attempt to put right the apparent
neglect of spelling in the junior and secondary schools,

but it is pathetic to have to read the spelling tips offered to young men who in two or three years will be qualified teachers. Here they are:

1. 'i' before 'e' except after 'c'.
2. Drop a silent 'e' before a vowel, but keep it before a consonant, e.g. 'coming' and 'advertisement'.
3. When building up words notice that double 'l' becomes single, e.g. 'fulfil'.

Such elementary spelling rules as these should, of course, be given to children at the age of ten or eleven, and indeed were so in all schools thirty or forty years ago before the doctrine of 'free uninhibited writing' crept insidiously into English education. In the back of the Collins' Standard Five Reader which I mentioned earlier, there are twenty-five pieces of dictation which were considered suitable for children of eleven in those far-off days of accuracy in written English. Here are some spellings which occur in the third passage of that book: banisters, proffered, preferable, pommel, asylum, minions, postilion, militia, allotted, sentinel, parley, colloquy, Coliseum, querulous, tranquillity, pacified, vermilion. I wonder what the percentage of misspellings would have been at that training college with some of these words. How would the students have fared with 'colloquy' and 'querulous'? Would they in fact have known what these words meant? Could they even pronounce them?

That average children of eleven in the 'bad old days' of dictation were expected to be better spellers than eighteen-year-old college entrants today may come as a shock to many people. They may even question if the pass at G.C.E. ordinary level in English Language which is laid down as an essential qualification for entry to teaching, is high enough to ensure that we do have cultured and competent teachers. It is true that since the last war the syllabus for G.C.E. English has become less demanding. There is now practically no formal grammar, and clause analysis, which certainly tested candidates' ability to understand the structure of a sentence, has also been dropped. There are now six grades of passing. Grade 1, the highest, is given for 70+ marks, while the lowest pass, Grade 6, requires only 45–49 marks. This means that a candidate can say he has passed G.C.E. English with a score of 45 out of 100, or 4½ out of ten, which is surely an abysmally low mark for a pass in such a certificate.

If the questions in the examination are difficult and the marking strict, then a 45 per cent pass mark may be justified, but from a survey of some recent English Language papers set by one of the boards, the questions do not appear very testing for young people who have at the age of sixteen received ten or eleven years of schooling. Question 3, for instance, in June 1968, gives 'pacify' for the expression 'calm down' and then asks for similar words ending in -fy for the five expressions: Make clear; turn into stone; alter fraudulently; frighten exceedingly; increase the apparent size of. The five words then have to be put into suitable sentences. If the finding of these five simple enough words is too difficult for the candidate, he can instead transpose a short passage from direct to indirect speech. It should be noted that words like clarify, petrify, falsify, terrify and magnify are the kind that would have appeared in a vocabulary exercise for an eleven-year-old thirty years ago, and a knowledge of direct and indirect speech would have been expected at the same age, as a glance at old school syllabuses will verify.

In the June 1969 Ordinary Level English Language paper of the same examination board, comes the following question: 'The following pairs of words are frequently confused. Write a sentence for each word (eight sentences in all) showing clearly how it differs in its meaning and use from the other word in the pair. Accept, except; insulation, installation; green house, greenhouse; outlay, lay-out.' It is most interesting to compare this question and its simple vocabulary with a question from an eleven-plus English paper of thirty years ago. Here it is: 'The following words have different meanings according to the way they are pronounced: contract, desert, object, permit, present. Use them in sentences of your own to show their meaning. You should write ten sentences.' I think it would be agreed that the eleven-plus question is very much more subtle and demanding than that from the G.C.E. paper, and of course it asks that the child taking it understands the functions of nouns and verbs.

Question 4 from the same paper asks the candidate to punctuate three short sentences in two different ways to give two different meanings. These are the sentences: (1) the bowler said the wicket-keeper ought to have held the catch. (2) i sold the car for £200 less than i expected. (3) what don't you understand. As an alternative to solving these exacting intellectual exercises, the candidate may rewrite in correct form three sentences, each of which contains two errors: (1) The result of the Grand National was quite different than we expected, and there were less horses running in it. (2) Mother is going for two weeks holiday, and the running of the house will be left to you and I until she returns. (3) The wines of Australia are as good, if not better than, South Africa.

Such exercises as these were set to children of ten or eleven thirty years ago, as reference to the text-books and examination papers of those days shows. Here is a typical question from an English paper set to grammar school entrance candidates in 1927. These children of ten or eleven were asked to: 'Explain exactly what is wrong with the following sentences and rewrite them correctly: (*a*) I am bigger than him. (*b*) Father said he would take you and I. (*c*) I don't know who the boy is like. (*d*) Each of the guests were given a present. (*e*) The lion what attacked his trainer was shot.'

The exercises for the G.C.E. Candidates today are of comparable difficulty to those set to eleven-year-olds in 1927, but there is this important difference. The G.C.E. Candidate can correct his given errors without properly understanding the grammar involved, but the little eleven-year-old of 1927 was asked to 'explain exactly what is wrong'. This requirement is obviously more demanding than the G.C.E. type of question, where the errors can be corrected by hit or miss methods, not necessarily based on a knowledge of language. In my view a General Certificate paper in English which does not require some evidence of language study is not exacting enough to serve as proof of fitness for teaching.

Some time ago, we had on school practice in my school a training college student who was an example of one who had been very ill prepared in the basics of English language, and yet had obviously gained enough marks in the G.C.E. Language paper to allow him to become a teacher. He was asked to prepare a lesson on the comparison of adjectives, and submitted to the class teacher his notes on this topic. He had given examples of the words he proposed to use with a class of nine-year-olds and had placed them in the traditional three columns marked Positive, Comparitive (*sic*) and Superlative. I might have been prepared to over-look the misspelling of 'comparative' but for the strange collection of words he had used for adjectival comparison. Among the familiar examples long, longer, longest; big, bigger, biggest; high, higher, highest; he had put 'run, running, ran; sleep, sleeping, slept; talk, talking, talked'. When I pointed out to him that run, sleep and talk were not adjectives he seemed puzzled and said, 'What's wrong with run, running, ran, and sleep, sleeping, slept? They sound all right to me.' It was clear that although he had obtained a pass of some sort in G.C.E. English Language, he hadn't any knowledge at all of basic English grammar, and did not even know the parts of speech. As well as I was able in a short time, I explained to him the functions of adjectives and verbs, and suggested that he should substitute adjectives for run, sleep and talk. He did this, but to my consternation I found that one of his new adjectival comparisons was 'little, littler and littlest'!

Clearly this student was ill-grounded in the understanding of his mother tongue, and while I would not claim that there are many as bad as he was, there are in my considered opinion far too many young teachers whose knowledge of the English Language is too superficial, largely owing to the slight demands imposed by the G.C.E. syllabus and the very low pass mark.

There are indications, too, that university undergraduates are no better grounded in their native tongue than are the teaching students. In 1967, the results of a survey, among 2,000 university entrants concerning their vocabulary, were published by Mr. John Kirkman of the Department of English and Liberal Studies of the

Welsh College of Advanced Technology. Students were asked to answer seventy-two questions about ordinary commonplace words like 'complacent' and 'dubious', and to make sure the selection was fair, these words were taken from scientific magazines, a quality newspaper, the *Listener* and a Somerset Maugham novel. Mr. Kirkman says the average student should have answered about sixty-five questions correctly, but the results for the different faculty groups were much lower than that. The averages were: Arts 55·5; Social Science 52·9; Pure Science 48·7; Applied Science 44·67; Agriculture 44·66; Philosophy 59·67, and Electrical Engineering 32·65. The words should not have been by any means difficult or unusual for people who on native intelligence and education came from the top 5 per cent of the population, and yet 47 per cent of arts students were unable to define 'synthesis'; 37 per cent of the applied scientists did not know that 'indolence' means laziness; 35 per cent of the pure scientists could not define 'lucid', and 62 per cent of the sociologists did not know the meaning of 'dissemination'. Mr. Kirkman's comments on the findings of his survey must be surely construed as a serious criticism of the standards of English which enable a student to enter a university. 'It is hard to see how anyone can comprehend or express subtle and complicated thoughts without a wide command of words. These test results suggest that many university entrants at present lack such a command.'

One trembles to think what the written English must be like of the 90 per cent of young people who do not aspire to be undergraduates or teacher training entrants, if so many of those who are chosen for this advanced form of education cannot spell, know no formal grammar and have such a restricted vocabulary. The universities have, from time to time, voiced their dissatisfaction with the appalling English of their entrants, notably in 1960, when a committee appointed by the Universities of Oxford and Cambridge examined the whole question and reported thus: 'The standard of English appears to us to be regrettably low, not only among the *majority* of candidates for admission to Oxford and Cambridge but also in the country as a whole.'

Six years before this, in 1954, the Ministry of Education had published a pamphlet called *Language*, which purported to make suggestions for teachers of English in primary and secondary schools. This pamphlet freely admitted that there were frequent complaints from employers about the spelling, punctuation and English composition of the young people who came from the schools to work for them. It further said that, although young teachers might consider criticisms from such sources unfair, after some years in the schools they would realise that these employers are not just grousing but have reasonable grounds for complaint. To quote from the pamphlet, 'These complaints are too general and have been going on too long to be no more than a grumbling kind of perfectionism. They are indeed no longer made only or mainly by local employers but also by very large organisations, including the Civil Service, which recruit nationally. They are made by the Forces also and by those who have to teach science students and even arts students at the universities and in post-graduate studies.' What an indictment of our educational system is contained in these admissions! And, let it be noted, they are from the very Ministry which is responsible to Parliament for the organisation of education in this country!

There is, however, in this pamphlet no admission that the falling-off in English language standards in the schools might have been set in motion by the exhortation in the 1937 *Suggestions to Teachers* to drop dictation from the syllabus and to remove formal grammar lessons from the time-table.

4

THE DECLINE IN ARITHMETIC

I mentioned earlier that I have gained a general impression, during my long school experience, of a decline in the standards achieved in the basic subjects and of a gradual slowing-down of the process of learning in the school-life of children. Some years ago I received unexpected confirmation of this impression when a parent asked to see me about the progress of her child, who was ten years old and coming up to the dreaded hurdle of the eleven-plus examination. This parent was concerned about her child's achievement in arithmetic, which she thought was lower than her own at the same age. I tried to allay her anxiety by my assurance that her child was not by any means backward in this subject, and that if the standard achieved by the average ten-year-old today did not seem to be as high as that of thirty years ago this was because we did not like hurrying the educational process, but preferred to delay the steps of learning until the child thoroughly understood each concept involved. However, she produced the actual eleven-plus exam. paper in arithmetic which she had taken in 1924, and below are some of the examples from it:

1. A centimetre of wire weighs 0·93 gramme. What is the length (to the nearest centimetre) of a piece weighing 100 grammes?

2. A bicycle wheel travels 7 feet 4 inches for each revolution of the back wheel. If the wheel revolves

twice in every second, at what rate in miles per hour is the bicycle travelling?

3. On a map on the scale of 6 inches to the mile a rectangular field appears as 1·7 inches long and 0·8 inch broad. Find in yards the length of fencing required to enclose it; and find the area in acres.

4. Divide 0·37044 by 0·0147

5. Simplify: $\dfrac{2\frac{1}{5} - \frac{1}{2} \text{ of } 3\frac{1}{3}}{3 + 1\frac{2}{5}}$

6. What is the rent at £3 10s. 0d. acre of a farm of 240 acres, 3 roods, 16 square poles?

7. A man bicycling at 10 miles per hour passes a man walking at 4 miles per hour. Twelve minutes later the bicyclist has a puncture. How far is he ahead of the walker when this happens? If the bicyclist takes 20 minutes to mend the puncture, will the man walking pass him while he is mending it or not? How far apart will the two men be when the bicyclist is ready to start again?

I had to admit frankly that my ten-year-olds would have found these examples difficult, but I explained, 'We are not so much concerned today with giving children long complicated sums. We prefer that they should fully comprehend the underlying principles of what may appear to be much simpler work.' My enquiring parent did not seem satisfied with this explanation, however, and gave it as her opinion that children in her day, through the rote-learning of tables and daily practice in doing long complicated sums, were given a much sounder grounding in the principles of arithmetic.

In my heart I was sympathetic to her point of view,

because as I have stated above, I feel that the standard of arithmetic has generally gone down in schools, and it is doubtful if the modern approach, with its emphasis on understanding rather than on quick mechanical accuracy, is providing children with a firm grasp of the four rules in number on which they can build their mathematics.

About eight years ago I received a visit from one of our old girls who had just completed her first year at a provincial teachers' training college. She was doing maths as her special subject, and wanted to see it being taken in school. She showed me the Mathematics Grading Test which had been set to all the new maths students on their entry to this college. This was a grading test which was being used so that the lecturer would know the capabilities of his students, and presumably such a test would be geared to the expected attainment of the average student being admitted that year. If the test were too easy or too difficult it would be useless from a diagnostic point of view, so we must suppose this lecturer set examples which he opined were within the compass of the average eighteen-plus young lady on her entry to teacher training. If I had needed any further proof of the low standards which are acceptable to those in charge of entry to the teaching profession, this maths grading test provided it. I have set it out in full, verbatim, because I think it should be of great interest to the general public, who probably think that intending teachers with a mathematical bent are able to cope with work of at least the General Certificate Advanced Level.

Here it is:

Mathematics Grading Test. Primary Group. Time 1 hour. Please show your working.

1. $6,453 + 7,483 + 7,962 + 5,948$

2. $7,009 - 5,436$

3. $9·756 \times 478$

4. £174 12s. 4d. ÷ 24. Give your answer to the nearest penny.

5. $2\frac{1}{3} + \frac{5}{12} - 1\frac{7}{8}$ 6. $1\frac{1}{2} \times \frac{4}{7} \times 1\frac{1}{6}$ 7. $1\frac{7}{12} \div 2\frac{3}{8}$

8. $15·8 \times 1·35$ 9. $4·56 \div 0·19$

10. A car running 22 miles to the gallon of petrol uses 14 gallons for a certain journey. How many gallons would be used for the same journey by a car which runs 28 miles to the gallon?

11. Find the cost of 8 yd. 1 ft. 8 in. at £1 19s. 3d. per yard.

12. A train travelling at an average speed of 39 m.p.h. can do a certain journey in 4 hours. How long would the same journey take at an average speed of 52 m.p.h.?

13. A lawn 50 ft. long and 25 ft. wide is surrounded by a path 4 ft. wide. Find the number of cubic feet of gravel needed to cover the path to a depth of 4 in.

14. The average age of 6 men is 37, and one of them is 42. Find the average age of the other five men.

15. The weight of a piece of wood 6 ft. long and $3\frac{1}{2}$ ft. wide is 40 lb. Find the weight of a piece of the same kind of wood 9 ft. long 2 ft. 4 in. wide and three times as thick.

16. Find what volume of water in cu. in. could be held in a rectangular tank 6·5 in. $\times$ 4·875 in. $\times$ 10 in. Give your answer correct to the second decimal place.

17. In a roll of print material there were 40 yd. Nine girls made themselves dresses, each taking $3\frac{1}{2}$

yds. of material. How much print was left in the roll?

18. When is ¾ of one whole A equal to ⅛ of another whole B?

19. How much change would there be from £1 after paying for 3½ lb. at 1s. 9d. per lb.?

20. Which is the faster train and by how much? the 11.25 a.m. arriving at 2.12 p.m. or the 11.48 a.m. arriving at 2.31 p.m.?

It will, I think, come as a shock to many people to compare what was expected of a child of eleven in 1924 with what is expected of an entrant to a certain teachers' training college forty years later. A number of the examples in the college grading test (Nos. 5, 6, 7, 9, 12, 14, 17, 19 and 20) are simple mental arithmetic sums which any child of ten or eleven between the wars would have taken in his stride, and it is, moreover, very strange to find that there is only one example, number 18, that could possibly be regarded as maths in the new sense. It should be noted, too, how very much more difficult is the second question on speeds in the eleven-plus paper compared with the feeble question which appears in the college entrants' test on the same subject. A comparison of the division of decimals questions in the two papers is equally illuminating; while the college entrant of eighteen-plus can get away with $4.56 \div 0.19$, which can be worked mentally, the eleven-plus candidate in 1924 had to cope with $0.37044 \div 0.0147$. Similarly, while question (5) in 1924 was a complex one on vulgar fractions, involving four arithmetical steps, the ones in the grading test for college, 5, 6 and 7 are ridiculously simple.

It would appear then from a comparison of these two examination papers that something has happened to

English education during the past thirty or forty years, and that standards in arithmetic have fallen considerably during that time. It has not gone unobserved by many teachers that this decline coincides with a period of persistent advice from inspectors and a host of amateur educationists that the rote-learning of the multiplication and other tables should be abandoned, that all arithmetic should be related to real life and therefore long cumbersome examples in the four rules should be eliminated, that knowledge of processes is more important than accuracy in mechanical arithmetic and that finally each child should progress at his own pace and never attempt new unfamiliar work until the concepts underlying previous work have been fully understood. No one, of course, can question the validity of this advice if teachers are not expected to deal with classes of forty and the children have all the time in the world to assimilate their arithmetical rules. It is, I conjecture, the too literal application of these teaching principles which has caused the sorry retardation of arithmetic achievement which the deplorably low standard of the teachers, grading test reveals.

It appears to me that so much attention has been paid to the advice to abandon rote-learning of tables and practice in mechanical arithmetic, that children nowadays have not the easy facility to deal with the ordinary calculation which is so essential to solving accurately the problems with which they are presented. If our backward teacher training entrants had learnt in their early stages of school life to deal quickly and successfully, albeit mechanically, with the basic arithmetical rules they would have found it much less tedious and frustrating to follow their college course now. Grounding in the four rules of arithmetic is the only satisfactory basis for a thorough understanding of mathematics. In Chapter 10 I hope to deal with the impact of the so-called 'new mathematics' on the English educational system.

5

THE OLD 'ELEMENTARY SYSTEM'
ITS STRENGTHS AND SHORTCOMINGS

When the First Parliamentary Reform Act was passed in 1832, the Duke of Wellington, who was much opposed to extending the franchise to the lower orders, is reported as saying: 'Now we shall have to educate our masters.' He meant, of course, that the people who were receiving the vote would have to be given the schooling necessary for them to exercise it properly. At that time all education in this country was through voluntary agencies, and it was not until the year after the First Reform Act that the Government made its first public grant, a mere £20,000, to be shared between two of the societies which were building and maintaining schools for the poor. In 1840, a Commission appointed to investigate the shocking conditions of child labour in mines and factories, discovered that the ignorance of these unfortunate children was as appalling as the conditions under which they were forced to work. It was estimated at the time that of the boys and girls of thirteen or fourteen, half could not read and three-quarters could not write, their only available form of schooling being the Sunday schools or those provided by the voluntary societies. After the Commission's report there was much agitation by liberal-minded people to make education compulsory, and eventually Mr. Forster's Education Act of 1870 did this for all children up to the age of ten. Subsequent legislation raised this to fourteen, and popularly elected school boards were created to supervise the newly built schools in areas where there was not already a school founded by one of the voluntary societies. It was from this first Education Act that the English Elementary System of Education sprang, and the people who had pressed for this reform did their utmost to ensure that the schooling provided in the new buildings was sound and efficient.

It was natural that in the early stages of the new compulsory schools the emphasis should be on teaching the children the basic elements of learning—reading, writing and arithmetic. These were considered, understandably, the beginning and end of schooling for those children who for the first time were compelled to come to school. They were regarded as the instruments for acquiring all knowledge, and so formed the basic foundations of the new elementary system of education. To ensure that there was a uniform pattern of schooling throughout the country, a Board of Education was created and standards of schooling were stipulated for each year of a child's school life. These standards were based on what an average child in each particular age group was expected to know, and promotion of children from one standard to the next was only made after they had been found by test to be proficient in the work of their present standard. It was a rigorous system, but it did provide a basic uniform standard of education for every child no matter in what part of the country he lived. If a child moved from a school in Devizes to one in Doncaster, or from one in Basingstoke to another in Burnham-on-Crouch, he would be placed in a class with a standard of work appropriate to his attainment in the three basic subjects of the curriculum, and moreover, he would find the work familiar, because it would be based on a syllabus which was generally common throughout the country. In those early days of the elementary system, promotion of children through the seven standards was not based on age. If a child could not pass the test for his grade he was left in that standard until he could. It was harsh treatment for those lacking in intelligence, but it provided a clear aim for the teacher and a spur for the child. The following log-book extract for 1886 from the school in which I work is illustrative of how the old standards system worked: 'Mrs. Mileham called and complained of her son being put back into the third standard, he having failed in arithmetic two years running. The mother called in the middle of last year to say that she would not have the boy pressed and that she would burn every home lesson he had, as he was quite forward enough and would have fits if troubled about his work. Under these circumstances it appeared to the master altogether inadvisable to endeavour to force the boy through the fourth standard, undoubtedly the hardest in the course of the school curriculum.' It would seem today very inhumane for the headmaster to talk of demoting a boy because of his inability to pass the Standard Four attainment test, and to use words like 'force the boy' would cause the progressives to hold up their hands in horror. However, the headmaster was only doing what all headteachers of those early days were compelled to do by reason of the 'Payment by Results' scheme under which they worked. At that time the State grant to a school depended on the yearly examination results. The annual examination was conducted by Her Majesty's Inspectorate, and on the performance of the children in the different subjects the grant was calcula-ted. In that same year, 1886, the annual report for our school was as follows: 'The boys have passed a very creditable examination in most respects, though both spelling and arithmetic are less thorough than they were last year. The points requiring attention are the spelling and the grammar of the second standard, the written arithmetic of the first, fourth and fifth standards and the mental arithmetic.

Fixed Grant.	4/6	
Singing.	/6	
Elementary		
Subjects.	7/–	
Grammar.	2/–	
Geography.	2/–	
Merit Grant.	2/–	(Good)
Total	18/–	

Total grant for year £83 14 0   ,,

As the Headmaster's salary depended on the grant, there was no doubt whatever that he would see that his school was efficient and that every child was stretched to the limit of his ability. Inspectors of education in those times were naturally regarded with fear, as their annual reports could make or mar a headteacher's reputation and, moreover, could affect him financially. On their visits to schools they would look carefully at the syllabuses of instruction to see if they were in line with general practice, and the questions set at examination would be based quite fairly on the material which the teachers claimed to be teaching. One of the most important documents in school was the time-table. This had to be produced on a standard form which showed each five minutes of the day as a square-space, so that at a glance the inspector could see the time allotted to each lesson. The five-minute squares so shown had to be added up for each subject and the results summarised on the time-table. It could thus be seen that, say, 200 minutes were given to Religious Instruction, 300 minutes to Arithmetic and perhaps 60 minutes to Singing per week. If the inspector did not think the amount of time allocated to a particular subject was sufficient he would indicate to the head that this should be changed in future. The time-table was considered so important in fact that it had to be signed by the head, agreed by the Managers, submitted to the local authority for signature and then finally had to be approved by the inspector. Any deviation from the time-table had, moreover, to be recorded in that other important document the school log book.

It was a rigidly unbending system, and it ensured that children were taught with a severity that would not be permitted today. It did, however, fulfil the aim which the originators of the elementary system intended—to teach the children of the poor the rudiments of learning, and moreover, in as cheap and uncomplicated a manner as possible.

It was a simple system, and this was its great strength. The children entered school at five years of age, and from then until they left at thirteen or fourteen their course of instruction was clearly mapped out. The facts to be learnt were plainly stated in the syllabuses for each class; there was a time-table which had to be followed; the assistant teachers were responsible for inculcating the facts at specific times, and the headteacher was responsible to the inspectorate for seeing that this tidy arrangement was carried out efficiently. It was indeed the kind of organisation at which the Victorians excelled. Like the English Civil Service, it was essentially orderly.

It was an authoritarian system, and everybody taking part in it knew exactly where he stood. The children were at the bottom, and so they were expected to be obedient and respectful to their teachers, who in turn through the head accepted without complaint surveillance by the inspectorate. Very large classes of up to sixty or seventy children could only be controlled by a firm discipline, and so direct instruction was the accepted pattern of education. It was a purely didactic method, with the teacher retailing facts from his store of knowledge, and by various means ensuring as far as possible that his pupils retained them. Because of the dreaded annual inspection, heads and teachers strove all the time to make certain that their pupils produced painstakingly neat and precise work in all subjects. Handwriting was taught systematically, and was quite naturally based on the calligraphy of the Civil Service. Great attention was paid to the loops and pot hooks of the letters so that a clear, flowing style was produced which had the additional advantage of being uniform throughout the country. Just as handwriting had to be clear and correct because it was the common means of communication, so had the words written to be set down in grammatical, punctuated form and as far as possible according to the rules of syntax. Written composition was an exercise in lucid expression, and although imaginative work was praised, ideas were considered secondary to the mode of setting them down.

In arithmetic the same philosophy of learning obtained. Figures had to be neat and orderly; sums had to be set down exactly; answers had to show a precise statement of the quantities and measures involved and, above all, they must be right!

In the other subjects of the curriculum children's

knowledge of facts was regarded as the criterion of successful teaching. If these were not remembered, then education had failed! In those days no teacher would have dared cover up his class's lack of knowledge by airily claiming to be offering the children a broad understanding of the humanities instead of them knowing the basic facts of history and geography. The reply to that argument would have been direct and simple—how can you understand any subject without knowing the facts?

It can be seen that the old elementary system was well organised, had definite aims, set itself standards and provided a means of checking that intention and achievement were as far as possible coincidental.

There were, however, certain shortcomings in the system. First, the 'payment by results' scheme was open to abuse, as it resulted in a narrowing of the curriculum to those subjects which were to be examined, and naturally headteachers made the annual tests the be-all and end-all of education.

Secondly, while the authoritarian nature of the schooling was in keeping with general opinion at the turn of the century, since that time there has been such a gradual change in the public's attitude to authority in general that a relaxation of the rigid discipline which was such a feature of the elementary school was inevitable.

Thirdly, although the uniformity of syllabus and teaching method was a great help in maintaining standards in the schools, it had a stultifying effect upon the development of new educational ideas, so that innovation of any kind was frowned upon. No one today would attempt to justify the 'payment by results' principle which activated the early elementary system of education, but nevertheless it did provide value for money. One of the Government supporters who was trying to justify it in a debate in the House of Commons is reported as saying, 'If education is expensive, it shall at least be good. If it is bad, it shall at least be cheap.'

This cynical remark shows how education was regarded at that time. It had to be efficient, but it must also be economical. We have come a long way since then to the present time, when we are prepared to spend vast sums on schools, colleges and universities, but there is not the same relentless scrutiny of the cost/efficiency of the education provided in these institutions. There has been a revulsion from 'payment by results' and a general relaxing of the authoritarian principle upon which school teaching methods were based. Educational doctrines are, of course, related to the social and political conditions of their times, and it is therefore not surprising that in the past fifty years there have been great changes in educational theory and practice. The reformers who have helped to bring these about have not only invoked the spirit of the age but have also used the arguments of educators and philosophers of previous centuries in order to revolutionise educational method. It is interesting to trace how the new ideas in education came about and to ask if they are entirely successful.

6

THE ROMANTIC INFLUENCE—
ROUSSEAU ET AL.

In the 1931 Report of the Consultative Committee on the Primary School it states: 'The curriculum is to be thought of in terms of activity and experience rather than of knowledge to be acquired and facts to be stored.' These momentous and oft-quoted words have had a very great effect upon English education, because they were a direct incitement to headteachers of primary schools to revise their traditional attitude to the teaching of young children. This idea of the child being the agent of his own learning rather than acquiring information compulsorily from a teacher in a set course of lessons, was not a new one. It had been recommended by a number of philosophers and educators at different times, but never until the Consultative Committee's Report did it receive the blessing of a favourable official pronouncement.

Long ago Plato said in *The Republic*: 'Knowledge which is acquired under compulsion obtains no hold on the mind . . . then do not use compulsion, but let early education be a sort of amusement.' This view, although emanating from such a revered source, did not receive much support until Rousseau, the French revolutionary thinker, revived the conception of a natural education in his famous book *Emile*, which was published in 1762. In this 'educational romance', the bringing-up of the boy Emile according to the so-called principles of nature is generally regarded as partly fictional and partly autobiographical. However, although it was not received with favour at the time it was published, and in fact angered the Church and offended the established social and political order, this book had a tremendous influence on educational thinking subsequently, not only in France but throughout the world.

Rousseau's main thesis in the education of his Emile was that what a child learns must come out of him by what he gleans from the experiences afforded to him, not by directly absorbing from teachers, knowledge which they have laid down for his improvement. This is how Rousseau would set about this seemingly difficult task: 'Let him know nothing because you have told him, but because he has learnt it for himself. Surround him with all the lessons you would have him learn without awaking his suspicions.' According to Rousseau, it is preferable to show a child how to discover truths for himself than teach them to him. 'Discovery methods' are better than didactic ones, and finding out by experience is preferred to verbal instruction. Rousseau's obsession with this theory and his dislike of contemporary pedagogy leads him at times to overstate his case. This is what he says: 'Give your child no verbal lessons; he should be taught by experience alone. Reading is the curse of childhood. When I get rid of children's lessons I get rid of the chief cause of their sorrow.' Rousseau goes on from this passage to advocate a postponement of book knowledge, and says rather petulantly, 'I hate books; they only teach us to talk about things we know nothing about.' He then makes a very intemperate statement, which may well have given the cue for all that has led to the modern view of 'reading readiness'. 'I am pretty sure Emile will learn to read and write before he is ten, just because I care very little whether he can do so before he is fifteen.' He next airily dismisses languages as among the useless lumber of education; states that history is beyond children's grasp and claims that geography is only learning the map.

These revolutionary sentiments of Rousseau, although coming from a man who had had little schooling himself, no experience at all of teaching classes of pupils and no children of his own, were to influence educational thought for the next two centuries to an extent which no other writer has achieved. Pestalozzi, the Swiss educationist, although he called *Emile* 'a highly impractical dream book', nevertheless acknowledged that it had had a most profound effect upon him. He compared the education which he had received both at home and in school with that which Rousseau wanted for Emile, and he came to the conclusion that, 'Home education as well as public education everywhere appeared to me to be exactly like a crippled figure which would be able to find a cure for its wretchedness in the fine ideas of Rousseau, and that it was there that it should seek this cure.'

Pestalozzi's method of teaching is expounded in his book, *How Gertrude Teaches her Children*, which was published in 1801. Like Rousseau, he believed that schooling should be according to nature and that the teacher's job should be to provide conditions for the child to grow like a plant according to its natural characteristics. Like a good gardener he should carefully tend it and by giving it the best possible state in which to grow, it would thrive and develop all its natural potential. It should never be forced. Pestalozzi was strongly opposed to traditional teaching methods which involved pushing facts into pupils under compulsion, often with the use of the cane. He was, however, in favour of maintaining discipline in school, and considered corporal punishment permissible if the teacher–pupil relationship was such that the latter would understand and therefore not be resentful. Unlike Rousseau, he did not believe that work and play were synonymous, but on the contrary, recognised that hard work was a special value in itself. In one letter to a colleague he wrote, 'As for your principle that one should make children work hard and that good instruction is indeed only to be achieved through hard work, I am in entire agreement with you.' He expected his own teachers to be able to arouse their pupils' interest sufficiently well so that an imposed discipline was unnecessary, but he would not have children distracted by noise under any circumstances, and in this feature of his method differed from other 'natural' educationists. He wrote this in 1798 about the home which he founded for homeless and orphaned children at Stans after the French had sacked the town: 'Silence as a means of inducing activity is the first secret of such a home. The silence which I demanded when I was there and was teaching helped me greatly to achieve my aim as did my insistence on pupils sitting up properly. By the silence I made it possible on those occasions when I demanded all the children to repeat after me, to hear every mispronunciation, and furthermore it enabled me to teach even with a soft, hoarse voice, not a word being heard other than that which I spoke and which the children had to repeat.'

Pestalozzi's educational efforts were experimental, as he himself admitted, but at least unlike his forerunner Rousseau, he did have practical experience in the classroom and found out that handling and controlling children were harder than writing about method. He is nevertheless not so well known as Rousseau, and until refugee schools in various countries were named after him, his name and work were certainly not renowned in England. He had, however, a very active disciple in the person of the German Froebel, whose Kindergarten Schools were common both in this country and on the Continent during the latter half of the nineteenth century. Rousseau had said of his Emile, 'Work or play are all one to him; his games are his work; he knows no difference,' and Froebel underlined this by stressing that play is the most characteristic activity of childhood. He is in fact so obsessed with this facet of child behaviour that he talks in very exalted terms about it. It is, he says, 'the highest phase of child-development— of human development at this period; for it is self-active representation of the inner from inner necessity and impulse'. He then goes on, after this rather abstruse statement, to glorify play in quite extravagant terms. 'Play is the purest, most spiritual activity of man at this stage, and, at the same time, typical of human life as a whole—of the inner hidden natural life in man and all things. It gives therefore joy, freedom, contentment, inner and outer rest, peace with the world. It holds the source of all that is good.'

This glorification of play was the basis of the Kindergarten idea for which Froebel is so famed. 'In the Kindergarten the children are guided,' so he said, 'to bring out their plays in such a manner as really to reach the aim desired by nature, that is to serve for their development.' Froebel, like Rousseau and Pestalozzi, was a romantic who believed that the child is by nature good, and that if allowed to develop naturally, 'without powerfully interfering influences', would choose what was most beneficial for healthy development. He says in his book, *Education of Man*, 'We must presuppose that the still young human being, even though as yet unconsciously, like a product of nature, precisely and surely wills that which is best for himself, and moreover in a form quite suitable for him.' This doctrine would seem to make the precepts of the parents and the instruction of the teacher quite unnecessary, because the child quite simply knows what is best for himself, but despite the naïveté of Froebel's child philosophy, he has had a very great influence upon English educational thinking, and a number of teacher training colleges have been founded bearing his name and promulgating his ideas.

Dr. Maria Montessori, who is the next significant figure in the movement away from a traditional, formal curriculum to an education which is alleged to be child-centred, was mainly concerned with the training of poor defective children in tenements in Rome. She was remarkably successful with these subnormal infants, and deduced from this that if the methods which she had employed with them were applied to normal children, then even more surprising results would be realised. Her method was a complete antithesis to the traditional formal type of schooling. Her assistants were not 'teachers' but 'directresses', and they had to abandon the normal didactic system of teaching. According to Montessori, a 'directress' must change her whole attitude to children. 'Instead of facility of speech she has to acquire the power of silence; instead of teaching she has to observe; instead of the proud dignity of one who claims to be infallible she assumes the vesture of humility.' Montessori did, it is true, train her pupils to work hard, but there was no actual imposition of a scheme of study, and no child was ever punished or rewarded. The most characteristic feature of her method was that class teaching was completely abandoned. Each child was considered as an individual and taught to develop as such.

Great as was the influence of Rousseau, Pestalozzi, Froebel and Montessori upon educational thought and practice, it was not till the American philosopher John Dewey postulated his theory of a completely 'child-centred' approach in school that English educationists began to urge a change in the traditional formal class teaching situation. John Dewey wrote a number of books on his educational theories, and because they were written in English and were therefore easily accessible and comprehensible, they exercised a great influence upon this country, which has been since the turn of the century very prone to accept and follow American thought and ways of life. Dewey had been greatly influenced by the continental educators who advocated activity and discovery methods and the abandonment of the old scholastic approach to education. He maintained: 'Proficiency and learning come not from reading and listening but from action, from doing and experience.' He was much opposed to children sitting in desks in class formation and being instructed by teachers. 'Force nothing on the child,' he says, 'give it free movement . . . let it go from one interesting object to another . . . we must wait for the desire of the child, for the consciousness of need.' Dewey's main criticism of the formal type of schooling which had been practised all over the world for centuries was, to quote him, 'its passivity of attitude, its mechanical massing of children, its uniformity of curriculum and method'. To meet these criticisms he wanted a change in educational thinking which would be like a 'shifting of the centre of gravity'. He could see signs of this coming, and describes it in the extravagant language of the romantics on the Continent who so influenced him. 'It is a change, a revolution, not unlike that introduced by Copernicus when the astronomical centre shifted from the earth to the sun. In this case the child becomes the sun about which the appliances of education revolve; he is the centre about which they are organised.' This rather poetical description by Dewey of his conception of the child as the sun about which educational matters should revolve gives the term 'child-centred' to the theory of education which he advocates. This theory has dominated both American and English thinking throughout the first half of this century, and must have played its part in the sentiment expressed in the quotation at the beginning of this chapter, which urges activity and experience as valid substitutes for the storing of facts and the acquisition of knowledge. It is interesting to examine if this idea of 'child-centredness' as a basis for practical classroom procedure is acceptable to most teachers, or to the parents whose children have been subject to the influence exerted by it.

7

THE WEAKNESS IN CHILD-CENTRED EDUCATION

I have tried to trace in the previous chapter, how the ideas of child-centred education and discovery methods came into English schools. Today—according to Lady Plowden, who chaired the Plowden Committee—as many as one in three primary schools in Britain are now fully committed to this method. The broad philosophy has affected many more.

There is no doubt that the thinking and writing of Rousseau and the other educators have made a great impact upon our whole educational system. Yet there have been other influential people besides the ones I have mentioned who have had their part to play in the propagation of the new methods, notably the sisters Rachel and Margaret McMillan, who were largely responsible for the development of the new nursery schools, Susan Isaacs, who wrote books for teachers about children learning through activity and experience, and Jean Piaget, who demonstrated that there are certain typical stages in children's intellectual development.

All these educators urged a greater flexibility in the school curriculum, and were united in their dislike of the formal and traditional method of teaching children. To achieve this desired flexibility, the normal school time-table with its restrictive, set divisions into subjects had to be modified, and greater freedom had to be given to the teacher to use the time at his disposal in any way he wanted. In many schools today the time-table has disappeared, except for a skeleton one, which merely indicates when such communal places as the hall, playing-fields or library are being used by particular classes, and leaves great blanks to be filled in any way the teacher pleases. When the time-table has gone there is not the same need for detailed schemes of work or syllabuses showing the ground the teacher should be covering, or indeed what the child should have learnt after a set period of time. Moreover, with both time-table and syllabuses disappearing from the school, heads and teachers find themselves relieved of the burdensome task of compiling them, so who can blame school staffs for welcoming the new progressive theories which seek to abolish the thraldom of the old-fashioned set programmes of work and learning?

How does the new freedom affect the children who have no longer to follow the dictates of a set time-table and curriculum? If we believe the advisers who have advocated the new freer methods and the headteachers who have responded to them, then working without the restraints of a set programme has been entirely beneficial. The Plowden Committee, which looked at a number of primary schools before issuing its report in 1966, was in no doubt about the desirability of the new progressive methods as opposed to the traditional formal ones. 'Towards Freedom of Curriculum' and 'Flexibility of Curriculum' are two very significant headings in a chapter in the report called *Children Learning in School*, and in reading it one feels that children who are still working to a planned set time-table are victims of a restrictive Victorian past. How much better it would be if they were offered the joys of learning through play, and were released from the bondage of an artificial curriculum! In Plowden, children's play is regarded as 'cultural', not 'natural', as is the play of animals. 'It often needs adult participation so that cultural facts and their significance can be communicated to children.' The anonymous Plowden writer who was responsible for these paragraphs on children's learning had evidently read his Froebel, and was convinced about play being 'the highest phase of child-development—the purest, most spiritual activity of man'. We are told that play enriches the lives of ordinary children and, to quote, 'Wide ranging and satisfying play is a means of learning, a powerful stimulus to learning, and a way to free learning from distortion by the emotions.'

This adulatory recommendation of the Play Way to learning in school is a feature of Plowden. The reader is left in no doubt where the sympathies of members of the committee lie. We are warned that 'rigid division of the curriculum into subjects tends to interrupt children's trains of thought and of interest, and to hinder them from realising the common elements in problem solving'. Having dispensed with the time-table and a fixed curriculum, Plowden readers are urged to try the 'free day' and something associated with it called 'the integrated curriculum'. There is no clear explanation of what this latter term means, but it seems that it is an extension of that other rather overworked idea 'the centre of interest'. This splendid phrase was much in vogue a few years ago when the progressives began to tire of that other fine term 'the project method', but there seems little difference in the way these systems of learning are applied. According to Plowden, 'The "centre of interest" begins with a topic which is of such inherent interest and variety as to make it possible and reasonable to make much of the work of the class revolve round it for a period of a week, a month or a term or even longer. Much of the work may be individual, falling under broad subject headings. One topic for the time being can involve both group and class interest, and may splinter off into all kinds of individual work.'

An example of this method working is shown in the report, and the description of the spontaneous reactions of the children to the given stimulus is very touching. The reader marvels at these responsive children who will work at so many different activities on their own initiative, and who will learn so much without direction from an adult. Here is the description of a typical example of the 'Centre of Interest' method of teaching. 'When a class of seven-year-olds notice the birds that come to the bird-table outside the classroom window, they *may* decide, after discussion with their teacher, to make their own aviary. They will set to work with a will, and paint the birds in flight, make models of them in clay or papier-mâché, write stories and poems about them, and look up reference books to find out more about their habits. Children are not assimilating inert ideas but are wholly involved in thinking, feeling and doing. There is no attempt to put reading and writing into separate compartments; both serve a wider purpose, and artificial barriers do not fragment the learning.'

How lovely and romantic all this sounds! How splendid for the children to decide of their own volition to embark upon these worthwhile pursuits without pressure from above! How satisfying for the teacher to watch from the side-lines, as it were, this unfolding and burgeoning of the buds of children's learning growth! Only a carping cynic would claim that all the spontaneous activities mentioned here—painting, craft, composition, reading and nature study—could have been undertaken probably more successfully under the direction of a teacher who had some predetermined aim, had prepared his formal lessons on the different topics and who was not subject to the chance whims and fancies of little children!

A serious student of 'centre of interest' methods, moreover, will no doubt ask whether it is realistic of those engaged in a very expensive education service to await the fortuitous descent of some birds to a food-table, or some equally random occurrence at school, to motivate a class of children to make models, paint, read and write on some interesting subject. The transient flitting nature of children's interests has long been recognised, and is pithily summed-up in Longfellow's famous line, 'A boy's will is the wind's will.' How indeed can anyone be sure that such a topic as that triggered off by the birds' arrival on the table will not perhaps develop into a series of spasmodic ventures into a whole variety of futile, unrelated activities which are time-consuming but valueless as true education? It is pertinent here to quote the Greek dramatist Aeschylus on the matter of birds and children. He said, 'The child pursues a flying bird', meaning that children left to themselves are likely to follow ineffectual and unprofitable courses, and this seems to be one of the dangers inherent in the 'centre of interest' method of teaching.

The Plowden Report concedes that when children pursue discovery methods there is a possibility that 'trivial ideas and inefficient methods may be "discovered"', but that does not deter the authors from vehemently advocating these methods. It is proudly stated in one paragraph of the report that a group of H.M. inspectors assigned to a certain area of this country in which some particularly good work is to be found, write as follows: 'The newer methods start with the direct impact of the environment on the child and the child's individual response to it. The results are *unpredictable* [my italics], but extremely worthwhile. The teacher has to be prepared to follow up the personal interests of the children who, either singly or in groups, follow divergent paths of discovery. Books of reference, maps, enquiries of local officials, museums, archives, elderly residents in the area, are all called upon to give the information needed to complete the picture that the child is seeking to construct. When this enthusiasm is unleashed in a class, the time-table may even be dispensed with, as the resulting occupations may easily cover mathematics, geology, astronomy, history, navigation, religious instruction, literature, art and craft.' Phew!—what a melange!

After this glowing description of children reacting to the impact of their environment, Plowden generously admits that the teacher needs perception to appreciate the value that can be gained from this method, although a layman might think that the advantages of such publicised modes of teaching should be apparent to all. It is also admitted that the teacher needs great energy to keep up with the children's demands, and yet one would have thought from the description above that all this youthful enthusiasm unleashed through interest would have made the teacher's task much easier. Surely this is the point of the exercise—the child through interest teaches himself, and the teacher watches benevolently from the touchline.

The plain truth is that 'centre of interest' or 'discovery' methods cannot be shown by any research findings to be in any way superior to the traditional formal way of teaching, however much the Plowden Report attempts to propagate their theories. They have, moreover, certain obvious disadvantages. The most fundamental and important weakness in the method is that the impetus for learning has to come from the child through interests which are allegedly awakened spontaneously by chance events or circumstances. There has to be no planning or predetermining of the lines which the discovery activity will take. The birds on the table outside the classroom window may set off a train of thought in the children's minds which will lead them into exploration and activities which have no intrinsic educational value whatever. The topic in fact may lead to the collection of trivia with no useful purpose in the learning situation, and the children may flit aimlessly and hopelessly about like butterflies in the rain. True learning connotes ordered planning. It cannot be achieved haphazardly or extemporaneously. It has to be acquired step by step in an ordered sequence.

The Plowden progressives who condemn the timetable for having restrictive divisions into subjects seem to have missed the whole point of compartmental arrangement. Teachers have always known that such subjects as history and geography are related, and have usually demonstrated this relationship to children, but there is such a large amount of specific material to be considered under each subject heading that it is both orderly and advantageous to treat the two separately. Correlation can, of course, be made when the teacher thinks it desirable.

It is strange that in the most advanced scientific age of all time we should be encouraging teachers to work without regard to a predetermined plan or system. Rousseau, who had had no scientific training and so was ill qualified to speak on the subject, said of his Emile, 'Let him not be taught science, let him discover it,' and it would seem that this strange advice is being largely followed by educationists today. Teachers are being urged to get their children out 'discovering' at all costs, and it would appear that any piece of knowledge acquired this way is more important than something learnt directly from a teacher. While no one would deny the value of discovery as a method of learning, it would be foolish to claim that facts are better learnt this way than by didactic methods. Is the child not to profit by what generations of scholars and discoverers have learnt before him? Must he learn everything first hand? If so, it will take him a lifetime to do it! As Professor Bantock has said so cogently on this subject, 'The notion that a child must follow through all the stages of human development under the steam of his own capacity to discover what his predecessors have already found out, is ridiculous. It is part of our human ability to be able to package, in assimilable form, information (concepts and relevant facts) which children can then digest at a rate which the original discoverers would have found astonishing. As we already have the structures, the job of the school is to find the best way of presenting them; and by "best" I mean also the most economical.'

In considering the economics of education, the most relevant factor is the size of class or what is more often called pupil/teacher ratio, because the salaries of teachers have the biggest bearing on the cost of schooling. Although during the past thirty years successive governments have done their utmost to reduce class sizes, the permissible number in secondary schools is thirty and in primary classes it is still forty. Actually, many classes in both types of schools exceed these stipulated numbers, but the cost of bringing them down to more manageable proportions makes the likelihood of it improbable. It is quite unrealistic to talk of children learning by 'discovery methods' when we are thinking in terms of classes of forty. Try if you can to picture this number of children deciding spontaneously to measure the area of an awkwardly shaped field at the back of their school, which is what Plowden suggests. See this horde advancing with surveyors' ranging poles, Gunter's chains, field notebooks and the other surveying impedimenta, and witness the teacher, like Froebel, gently urging them on to the joys of purposeful activity! It is an enchanting picture, but not at all realistic! We must face the unpleasant fact that with a class of forty ten-year-olds, the measuring of an irregularly shaped field by triangulation is a very difficult undertaking. It might be done with a group of intelligent children who did not exceed ten in number, but even then they would need a considerable amount of time spent in preparation, and they would require also a good understanding of basic arithmetical rules before such a task could be successfully carried out.

This question of class sizes is the crux of the argument about the practicability of 'child-centred' education. To get classes down to the manageable number for 'centre of interest' or 'discovery' methods to work, say fifteen children per teacher, would certainly overstretch the capacity of the teacher training colleges, and even if the number of extra teachers could be found, payment of their salaries would bankrupt the economy. This is a plain statement of the economic facts of state education in this country. Classes cannot be substantially reduced in size because it is too costly.

It is therefore rather ridiculous for Plowden Reporters and other progressive educationists to advocate 'informal' methods of teaching, and it is also very irritating to teachers engaged in the state educational system to see such methods recommended. In the middle of the Plowden Report there is a collection of photographs intended to illustrate the happy, informal nature of modern 'activity' methods in junior schools. It is a clever piece of propaganda which begins with a photograph of a class of little children in a typical pre-war council school. There are thirty-six children seated at what used to be called 'dual-desks'. The desks are in orderly rows, and the children are seated at them in orderly fashion. The picture is called 'Children at Work 1937', and despite the constraint of orderliness, they look as happy and bonny a set of little boys and girls as you would see anywhere. Underneath this picture is another, showing children at work in 1966, and it is clearly intended to be a favourable contrast with the earlier one. These modern children are in what is called an 'open-plan school', which appears to be a series of small rooms joined by a wide passage of about six feet. There are about ten of these open-sided rooms, and children can be seen in them seated at tables apparently doing some form of hand-work. It all looks very jolly and informal in the best modern vein, but the significant thing is, that in a space possibly five times as big as that of the 1937 classroom, only eleven children can be counted. Modern methods, it appears, need few children and much space!

This is borne out by reference to the other pictures in this series. In Plate 4, for example, a lovely, young, blonde schoolmistress is shown seated on a log reading to five little children, also sitting on logs. This delightful idyll is entitled, 'Listening to a Story'. In Plate 5 another young teacher is helping three children to do some modelling. This is called 'Experimenting with Clay'. Opposite this picture is one of a fetching young teacher seated on the floor with six small children who appear to be reading. The teacher is pointing to one of the books and the caption says 'An Incentive to Read', although what the incentive is does not seem very clear. Perhaps having the fetching young teacher on the floor with them is an inducement to reading readiness. It does not say.

Now in all these pictures, which are obviously posed for a good photographer, the number of children 'at work' rarely exceeds five or six. This tempts the average primary school teacher to pose the question, 'Where are the other thirty-five?' Perhaps they are absent sick, or maybe they are in another part of the building being taken by a traditional formal type of teacher who was not chosen as part of the progressive Plowden propaganda. We shall never know about this, but I am certain that when most teachers of forty children see these pictures they feel as I do, that Lady Plowden and her committee are leading us up the educational garden path. These lovely glossy prints seem rather phoney— something of a confidence trick in fact. They come in the same category as the I.T.A. commercials, where the hound Rufus always manages to select the food which contains the marrow-bone jelly with added vitamins.

Classes in primary schools are never five or six in size, and therefore activity or discovery methods are never a practicable proposition. A teacher who tries free informal methods with classes of forty is heading for disaster. We have already noted that Rousseau, who through his book *Emile* advocated the shifting of educational emphasis from the curriculum to the child, had no children of his own, no schooling to speak of and no experience of class-teaching. John Dewey, the American educationist, whose conception of 'child-centredness' so dominated educational thinking throughout the first half of this century, unlike Rousseau had been involved in the founding of a school, but this was no ordinary run-of-the-mill affair. Dewey's Laboratory School was attached to the University of Chicago and in pupil–teacher ratio was as favoured as the lucky participators in the idyllic pictures in the Plowden Report would appear to be. The Dewey School started in 1896 with sixteen pupils and two teachers. When it closed in 1904 there were 140 pupils, a full-time staff of twenty-three and ten part-time assistants. Without the part-timers this works out at one teacher to six children and with them, one to four. This is child-centredness indeed. It must have been comparatively easy to provide both teachers and children with books, and with logs to sit on!

Let us not be taken in therefore by all the fervent propaganda of the Plowdenites and the many other dilettanti who urge us to abandon the old formal methods of teaching which produced the high scholastic standards for which this country used to be renowned. If the experimental discovery methods are claimed to be more congenial for children and also more effective agents in the learning process, then let there be some Ministry-controlled research on their effect in a number of schools in different parts of the country. Let this research be in the hands of experienced teachers, and let it extend over five years with independently conducted tests at the end of this period. It is, of course, true that there has been some research in America on discovery methods, but many of the findings made there were contradictory. It is perhaps significant, however, that in the country where Dewey's child-centred philosophy was born and was so uncritically accepted there should now be growing doubts expressed about its validity.

Professor Bantock, who is Professor of Education at the University of Leicester, and who has examined various teaching methods with an impartial eye, issued a warning note to English educationists when he recently wrote, 'It must indeed be said quite categorically that the superiority of discovery methods cannot at present be justified on the grounds of empirical research. Therefore, the teacher must rely on his own experience of what is effective, and not allow himself to be *bullied by dogmatists* for the new order.'

Teachers are indeed too easily influenced by amateur advisers, and are generally too prone to innovate for innovation's sake. Because much of their work is of necessity dull routine, and basically repetitious, they are tempted to chase after every new hare started from the educational undergrowth, whether it be painting on cheese-rind, music-teaching through rubber-bands, the artistry of toilet-rolls or just the jolly new mathematics. Such diversions bring a temporary excitement to both teachers and pupils, but in the long run, if children are to progress satisfactorily, the daily systematic and formal approach to lessons must be made. There is no escape from this! However deeply rewarding a task, teaching is a hard grind, and no attempt to transform it into happy informality can ever be successful.

8

THE FAILURE OF THE LOOK-AND-SAY
READING METHOD

A parent came to see me recently about the progress of his ten-year-old son who was soon to take his eleven-plus examination. After our interview he talked to me about the lad's little sister, who would be entering my school when she had reached the transfer age. He was concerned that she did not seem to have any knowledge of the sounds of letters. The evening before when father came home from work, this little girl had said to him proudly, 'Daddy I can spell your name!' Father was pleased of course and said, 'All right dear, let's hear it,' whereupon Gillian spelt, 'MUMMY'. Now Dad, who himself had been reared on systematic drill in letter-sounds, in the 'bad old days' of alphabetic or phonic reading methods, could not understand how his little girl had no knowledge of building words from the sounds which the letters make. To him it was inexplicable that DADDY could be confused with MUMMY, but to anyone who knows anything about the 'Wholeword' or 'Look-and-say' method of teaching reading, the explanation was simple enough. Gillian had been taught in her school to associate whole words with pictures of the persons or things which they represented. She had seen flash-cards, as these pictures are called, with representations of many common objects, displayed around the classroom walls, and with daily association of these with the printed words it was fondly hoped that this little girl and her classmates would be able to recognise words like mummy, daddy, door, window, brother and sister whenever they saw them. The shapes of the words would become so familiar in fact that eventually, when the pictures were withdrawn, the children would be able to distinguish them easily and accurately.

We have seen how ineffective this whole-word method of reading can be, and in a previous chapter it was shown how reading experts like Keith Gardner and Betty Root are of the *opinion* that children nowadays are taking longer over the process of reading than they formerly did, despite the many lovely picture-book schemes available. Mrs. Root reminds us that there are no less than thirty-four different reading schemes published in England and America, but a multiplicity of methods does not seem to have achieved satisfactory reading results. In the Ministry of Education's publication *Language* it is freely admitted on page 166, 'For some years the trend in this country and in the United States of America has been for children to begin reading at a later age than formerly—at an age of about six and a half years.' This was in 1954, and according to the two reading authorities quoted above, the position has become worse since then, and reading has been delayed still further. The tragedy of this late start in children's reading is that a number of children of superior mental ability, say 10 per cent of the population as a whole, are actually two to three years advanced in intellectual potential, and therefore should be reading at a very early age indeed. The Ministry's report, moreover, warns about this neglect of able children in these words: 'There has been a tendency sometimes to forget that *some* children (a few) have a mental age of six to six and a half years when they are four to five years old, and are mature, not only intellectually, but in other ways. A *considerable proportion* of children have reached maturity in all these ways by the age of five to six years. While there may be a greater danger of introducing some children to reading prematurely than of delaying introduction for some who are ready, there is no purpose in delaying instruction for those who *are* ready.'

The thirty-four different published systems of teaching reading which have been mentioned are not thirty-four different basic methods. They are simply versions of the four fundamental methods which have been used at various times since the skill of reading has been taught in schools. These are the Alphabetic, the Phonic, the Whole-word or Look-and-say and the Sentence methods. The Alphabetic Method, as its name implies, was based upon a knowledge of the letters of the alphabet, and words were built up by spelling out these letters by name. It was a laborious process, and much parrot-like repetition was needed to ensure its success. It was particularly suitable for dealing with the huge classes which were common at the beginning of the elementary system of education, when strict discipline and obedience were demanded from children. It was a successful system, and thousands of children at the end of the nineteenth century and the beginning of this one were taught to read by this method. Because it built up words from letters, we call this way of teaching reading a synthetic method. It was eventually superseded by a similar method based upon the sounds not the names of the letters, which we call the Phonic System. This method had one great advantage. When children had learnt to build up words from the sounds of their constituent letters they could easily pronounce new words without any help from their teachers. For many years the phonic method held the field in England and America as the recognised means of teaching children to read, and was also the normal reading procedure for those countries whose spelling is almost wholly phonetic, like Germany and France.

Synthetic reading methods, like the Alphabetic and Phonic systems, do of course demand much hard work and dedication from the teachers, because the sounds of the letters have to be remembered by the children, and this involves much repetition, which can be sheer drudgery for those engaged in the operation. However, when children have mastered the letter-sounds they can proceed to build up unfamiliar words and find no difficulty in learning to 'bark at print', which is the derogatory term used by critics of the phonic system of reading.

Whether it was the alleged drudgery associated with phonics teaching, and the attraction of a new method which would make things easier for both teacher and taught, or just the fact that America had gone completely over to a new reading approach is not certain, but it is a fact that after the First World War the 'Look-and-say' method gradually infiltrated into English schools, and eventually took them over. This method begins with the display on cards or sheets of paper of whole words which are associated with objects, or with pictures of persons or things. Children, instead of being concerned with letters and their sounds, have to remember the look and shape of whole words. With the Sentence Method, whole sentences and phrases are displayed, which children are expected to remember, and these can eventually be broken down into component words. Look-and-say is considered more attractive for children than Phonics, because it is claimed that from the start they can be introduced to more interesting material than is available to the latter method. Whole words and phrases, it is said, are more exciting than dull letter sounds. However, Look-and-say readers can be just as repetitious as phonic primers, because each reader has a 'sight-reading vocabulary' which is fixed. If children are reading by Look-and-say it is necessary that in the first reader used there shall be a fixed number of words, say 300, which form the basis of the stories in that book. This is called a 'controlled' vocabulary, and consists of only the words with which the children have by that time been made familiar by their use of flash-cards. Trying to write interesting stories with a strictly limited vocabulary is very difficult, and so we get some pretty dull stuff, with the 'controlled' words repeated as often as possible. Usually the story material is about a boy and a girl called Sam and Sue or Mick and Mary, and these children have exciting times at home, in the garden or at the farm. The illustrations are profuse and the number of words few on each page. The readers are beautifully produced, but the gaiety of the pictures is spoilt by the scantiness of the vocabulary. The known 'sight' words are repeated over and over again. Here is a typical piece of reading from such a book.

> Sam said, 'Go, Go.
> Go and see.
> Let us go and see.'
> Sue said, 'No, No.
> Run, Sam, Run.
> Run to Mum.'

It is difficult to see how writing like this can be said to be more exciting than the lists of letter-sounds which had to be learnt under the phonic system. The second reader in a Look-and-say system such as this will contain the 300 words of the first reader plus 300 new words, so that the writer will now have 600 words to play with in writing some more similar exciting pieces about Sam and Sue. It need hardly be said that Book Two is not much more thrilling than Book One, except that Sam and Sue find themselves in some new situations, and there are some new words to be repeated over and over again besides the ones from Book One. The third reader will introduce a further 300 words, and the fourth reader another similar number, so that eventually the children will have had experience of no less than 1,200 words, but there will have been endless repetition of the words in all four readers in an effort to familiarise the children with their shapes, because by the look-and-say method they are not able to say them by the sounds of their constituent letters.

Now this whole-word method of reading is not based on any sound principle which can be explained to a child. He can only be asked to observe the general pattern of configuration of a word or to note any special characteristics which it may have. His attention might be drawn to its similarity with some other word, or he might be shown that parts of it are like parts of another word with which he is already familiar, but it will be a very skilled teacher indeed who can point out such features of words to a young reader. Advocates of Look-and-say will sometimes point proudly to the fact that little Willie can recognise a difficult word like 'elephant' or 'chimpanzee', but if his basic method of word-recognition is solely by noting the general configuration of those words, then the substitution of, say, 'elevator' and 'chinchilla' will probably bring the wrong responses. The boy who has been taught the phonic approach, however, will be much more likely to recognise such polysyllabic words as these by breaking them up into their syllables and sounding them.

Phonics is a logical method of learning to read, because it uses the sounds which the letters of the alphabet make to build up words. Before there was an alphabet there was picture-writing, where every object was represented by a picture. The word 'lion' was shown by the drawing of lion, the word 'man' by a picture of a man, the word 'boat' by a sketch of a boat. Each word therefore had a different pictorial representation, and although in time men learnt to make these symbols simpler and simpler, a vocabulary of 10,000 words needed no less than 10,000 pictures to represent it. There was no escape from the drudgery of memorising these 10,000 picture-symbols, until the alphabet with its twenty-six letters and forty-four sounds allowed the pictures to be replaced by letter-symbols. Words could then be written by breaking them down into sounds and representing them by the letters which made those sounds. In order to read and write you simply had to memorise the sounds of all the letters in the alphabet. It was therefore understandable that teaching of reading from the very beginning in all languages was alphabetic/phonetic in character and was concerned with the building up of words. Why such an obviously sound method of teaching reading should have been replaced by the Look-and-say or Word-method is incomprehensible, but clearly the advocates of the new system must have thought that their way was better. The idea started in America, where in 1881 a book was published called *The Sentence Method of Teaching Reading*. This recommended that children should be trained to recognise whole phrases and words from the beginning, instead of building up words from letter-sounds. The method soon caught on, and by about 1920 the phonic method had practically disappeared from American schools. Britain soon followed America, and between the years 1920 and 1930 Phonics gradually began to disappear from our educational scene, so that by the end of this period, Look-and-say reigned supreme in many of the schools in this country.

It is rather ironic that in 1931, when Look-and-say had established itself firmly as the fashionable system, the Board of Education's Consultative Committee on the Primary School should issue the statement to which I referred earlier, 'The process of learning to read should be nearly finished by the time the pupil reaches the age of seven. The mechanical difficulties will then have been overcome by most of the children.' This pious hope was, of course, based on observation of schools during the previous ten years, when phonics was still being used in Britain, and the baleful effects of the whole-word method had not been fully felt. The members of the committee could not, of course, have been expected to know that the next two decades would show a progressive decline in reading ability in schools, so that by 1954 it would be officially admitted that six and a half years was the normal age to *begin* reading in Britain and America.

As we have seen, the whole-word method of reading or its extension, the sentence-method, is based on the belief that children can memorise whole words and phrases by seeing them presented in association with objects or with pictures of objects. While it is true that children are capable, through constant repetition, of being able to recognise the whole shape of many words, if they are ever to learn to read with an extensive vocabulary they will have *at some stage* to be given some basic training in the sounds which the letters make. In other words, they will eventually have to turn to phonics to become accomplished readers. Moreover, Look-and-say has an inbuilt disadvantage in comparison with phonics in that it does not help children to spell correctly. Indeed, it is certainly partly responsible for the parlous state of English spelling in our schools and colleges.

I have referred in Chapter 3 to the deplorable spelling deficiencies shown by students in a teachers' college of education. While much of the blame for these is no doubt attributable, as I have said, to the thoughtless injunction from teachers not to bother about spelling or grammar, but to write copiously and without restraint, doubtless, equal blame attaches to the Look-and-say method of teaching reading. If, as probably is the case, many of the students at this and other similar colleges were trained in reading through whole-word methods, then they have some valid excuse for writing words incorrectly. It is likely that of those students who could not spell 'business' (21 per cent), many wrote it as 'buisness'; of those who failed on 'tragedy' (31 per cent), many put it 'tradegy'; and it is certain that of the 35 per cent misspellers of 'definite', many called it 'definate'. Such errors as these are caused by the readers not breaking up the words into syllables and pronouncing them separately. No one who had been trained to read phonetically could write 'tradegy', or 'buisness', because the wrong syllabic sounds would indicate the misspellings. Under the whole-word system, however, it is so easy to confuse words of similar configuration. Dr. Rudolf Flesch, who wrote a best-seller on the bad effects of Look-and-say reading methods in America, gives a list of thirty misspellings which he calls 'the current campus favourites', They include 'buisness' and 'tradegy', 'Febuary', 'libary', 'suprise' and 'Britian', all of which would be spelt correctly by a phonic-trained reader. Dr. Flesch's book, *Why Johnny Can't Read*, puts all the blame for the deterioration in children's and students' standards of reading and spelling fairly and squarely on the Word-method of teaching reading. He maintains that whole-word methods are just a form of word-guessing, because they are not based on the systematic knowledge of letter-sounds which is the only true basis for learning to read. He ridicules the repetitive text of the early Look-and-say readers with their feeble limited vocabulary, and maintains that the effect of the restrictive use of 'controlled' words reaches to the highest stages of education. This is what he says on the subject: 'We have long since reached the point where we reduce not only the vocabulary of all readers in the first six grades, but also the vocabulary of all text-books in other subjects, of junior-high-school books, of senior-high-school books, and now even of some college texts. Everybody today accepts it as gospel that all books for children and adolescents have to be thinned, watered, diluted. We do not dare any more to expose our children to normal English.'

This view of American shortcomings in reading ability due to Look-and-say is underlined by a comment from Mr. John Duncan, O.B.E., in the British Ministry of Education's pamphlet *Language*. 'No widely circulated reader in the U.S.A. in recent years has any phonic basis nor contains any phonic work. During the past two years there have been signs of reaction. Some American educational journals have been noting protests from employers of labour who complain that many workers in factories are unable to read notices which contain semi-technical words, even when these words are in common use in their speech. The printed words are new patterns not previously seen, and these people (possibly of below middle-ability) are unable to analyse and synthesise them.' This last sentence exposes the weakness of whole-word method. Reading by this means is merely trying to remember patterns or shapes. It is not a logical build-up into words of the sounds which the letters form.

It is asserted by the exponents of look-and-say that phonics is unsuitable for teaching English children to read, because English is not a phonetic language. While it has to be admitted that English contains a number of irregularly sounded words like 'plough', 'trough', 'through' and 'though', which must confuse anyone learning the language, there are only about 13 per cent of English words which are irregular in spelling. The other 87 per cent follow definite rules. Moreover, English has tremendous advantages over the phonetic languages such as French and German in that it has no inflexions to speak of, no gender of consequence and little formal grammar. These favourable factors in our language more than compensate for the irrationalities of our 13 per cent unphonetic words. It is surely not asking much to expect English boys and girls to remember 'wood' and 'would', 'bough' and 'bow', 'won' and 'one' and 'to', 'too' and 'two'? I have always found children amused by these strange vagaries of our language and not at all unwilling to show that they know how to distinguish between them. French children must have a much harder task with their gender of nouns and adjectives and their tiresome inflexional irregular verbs, even though their pronunciation is more rational. I have found over many years of teaching English to foreigners in further education centres that *au pair* girls from a number of continental countries have no difficulty at all in picking up our language, because they find its general structure simple and the absence of inflexions encouraging. They are, it is true, puzzled by our spelling irregularities, but welcome prepared dictation as an aid to smoothing them out. It is noticeable that although in the early stages of learning to read English they not unnaturally make 'laughable' mistakes in pronunciation, they are at least able to tackle strange words from their familiarity with their own phonetic systems. They do not have to guess at whole-words, like English children who have been trained on Look-and-say.

Now to someone outside of the educational service it must seem strange that the alphabetic/phonetic system used in Britain until after the First World War, and which had proved so successful in teaching several generations of English children to read, should be abandoned in favour of the whole-word method which we have seen has prolonged the time taken in acquiring reading skill. A layman would imagine that the Ministry of Education, the Inspectorate and the teachers would long since have got together, and by careful research have determined which of the known methods of reading was the best. It is true there has been some small, half-hearted research on the matter by private investigators, but nothing definite has emerged from these studies. Dr. Vernon made a summary of previous findings on the subject in 1957, and considered that the complexity of the reading problem arises from 'the vagaries of fashion in teaching methods, the difficulty of defining exactly what each method includes and the impossibility of assessing exactly the skill of the teachers who employ the methods'. It is certainly true that the 'vagaries of fashion' more than anything else bedevil the search for a consistently successful method of teaching reading. So many schemes and so many variations of method pour out from the educational presses that the average teacher is bemused and bewildered by the vociferous claims of the authors and the publishers who are busily pushing the sales of their products. In 1969 Dr. Goodacre issued a comprehensive list of the known published reading schemes in use in this country. She has classified them as based on Look-and-say, Phonic and Mixed, the latter term meaning that the schemes under this heading use a mixture of the two main methods. Of the thirty-four schemes so described, no less than thirteen rely on Look-and-say, six are Phonic-based, while fifteen claim to be using the Mixed method. It would seem from these figures that the Word-method, despite the criticism it has received both in America and this country, is still the most popular method, but it would also seem that a large number of publishers and their followers are attempting to combine the two main ways of teaching children to read by starting with Look-and-say and introducing Phonics later. One can imagine the bewilderment of heads and teachers who are trying desperately to find a true path to follow amidst the present confusing maze of reading methods and materials.

The confusion has been made worse recently by the claims put forward by the adherents of Sir James Pitman's Initial Teaching Alphabet method of teaching reading. This much-boosted means of teaching is based on the use of forty-four characters to represent the number of sounds in the language instead of the traditional twenty-six. Small letters and capitals are distinguished only by size. It is claimed that when young children are presented with these forty-four unambiguous characters they pick up reading skill much more quickly, and have no difficulty in transferring to the traditional orthography when ready. I.T.A. started about eight years ago and has been tried in some 3,000 schools, which is about one-tenth of schools in this country. A recent report sponsored by the Schools Council came out much in favour, and said that widespread use of Sir James Pitman's system would raise the standard and rate of children's reading progress. There were some reservations, however. The evidence in the report indicated that after three years of schooling the reading attainment of most children taught in the traditional way was approximately equal to those who began their reading through I.T.A. This poses another question for bewildered teachers. Shall they adopt I.T.A. or stick to their most recent choice from the other thirty-four miscellaneous systems? No one can answer this question for the teachers, who are further confused by the existence of still more aids to reading, such as Dr. Gattegno's Words in Colour and Mr. Kenneth Jones's Colour Story Reading, which make choice of methods even more difficult.

How does all this apparently prodigal wealth of reading aids and methods affect the teachers in training? How can they know which is the best reading method and the one they are most likely to find in school? One would suppose that the teaching of reading by all methods would be a main part of the course in all teacher training establishments, and that familiarity with Phonic, Look-and-say, I.T.A. and words in colour schemes would be acquired by every primary school student by the time of leaving college. This, however, is not the case. Very few training college students are given systematic instruction in the teaching of reading, so that the young probationer in a junior or infant school has to pick up the information for herself. Dr. Joyce Morris, who carried out a very full survey of standards of reading in Kent primary schools in 1953, found that although about 45 per cent of the children transferring from infant to junior schools at the age of seven-plus still needed the kind of teaching associated with the infant school at time of transfer, approximately 75 per cent of the teachers taking these children in the transition classes had no training in infant methods whatever, 52 per cent had no experience in an infant school, and about 18 per cent of them were neither familiar with infant methods nor had any knowledge of how to teach beginners reading. As a further comment on the same subject, Dr. Morris, perhaps the leading authority on reading in this country, stated at a Cambridge conference in 1969 on the professional preparation of teachers for teaching reading that 'only 35% of students following infant courses had satisfactory training in the teaching of this subject, and over 22% were given no specific information at all' on this most vital of all subjects in the school curriculum.

This staggering announcement from an authority on reading, whose research was carried out under the auspices of the National Foundation for Educational Research, was further underlined at the annual conference in 1969 of the National Association of Head Teachers, where Mr. James Rudden, headmaster of Bishop Thomas Grand Comprehensive School, Streatham, proposed the setting up of a working committee to investigate the output of teachers 'inadequately prepared in fundamental teaching skills and responsibilities'. He maintained that more than half the teachers in primary schools had not been trained to teach a child how to read. 'Not only that. More than half the pupils coming into Junior schools suffer very real reading difficulties. Government policy has been to provide lots of teachers, but has quantity been at the expense of quality?' There was a loud 'Yes' from the delegates at this conference, and to show full agreement with Mr. Rudden's opinion, the delegates passed by 428 votes to 2 a motion demanding an immediate investigation into the teaching methods of colleges of education.

That student teachers in training colleges should not be trained to teach reading must come as a shock to members of the public. It is rather like hearing that a doctor has not been trained in anatomy, or that a butcher's apprentice has not been shown how to cut up meat. However, the whole story of English education in the past thirty years is one of muddle, mismanagement and neglect.

The parent who was worried about his little girl confusing MUMMY and DADDY did not know, of course, that there are nearly forty schemes for teaching reading in schools, and that teachers are confused by the multiplicity of methods from which to choose. He did not know that many junior and infant teachers leave college after three years' training without having been given adequate instruction in the use of reading methods. Finally, he did not know that Look-and-say could never show Gillian how to distinguish between MUM and DAD without the aid of picture-clues, simply because she had not been told about the sounds which the letters make.

In her book, *The Challenge of Reading Failure*, published in 1968 as a further comment on the National Foundation's investigation into reading standards in Kent,

Margaret Cox makes the following important observation: 'Schools which used a formal, systematic approach to reading in the reception class, basing their instruction on a primer, seemed to produce better readers than the more permissive schools, and schools which undertook phonic instruction with five-year-olds produced better results, at least with children of average and below average ability.' It would seem from this statement that a return to the Phonic method of teaching reading in a traditional, formal school situation might be long overdue!

9

THE NEED TO COMMUNICATE
THE RIGHT WORDS IN THE RIGHT ORDER

One of the most noticeable features accompanying the movement in schools towards child-centred educational theory has been the loud demand for self-expression in infant and junior schools. As teaching has moved from class instruction to individual work, so has emphasis been placed on encouragement for the child to express himself freely in art, craft, drama, and oral and written English. Moreover, because it is widely held that constraint of any kind from the teacher inhibits self-expression, it is urged that aid given to children in the acquisition of skills should be wholly incidental. Now, while this view may be valid in the case of manual skills, such as art and craft, where the child may be safely allowed to pick up his dexterity as he goes along, it is not by any means sure that this course can be satisfactorily followed with written English. Both oral and written English are basically means of communication, and if those who are indulging in self-expression wish to command an audience, then they must talk or write in a conventional idiom which can convey to others the thoughts and ideas in their minds. It is not enough to prattle like a baby formlessly and incoherently. If self-expression is to make impact on the listener or the reader it must conform to the generally accepted language of the community. In other words, it must observe the rules of syntax. It is in this respect that in my view much of our modern teaching of English fails. In its enthusiasm for free uninhibited written and oral expression, it neglects attention to the skills of accuracy in grammatical construction which would make the speech or writing more effective.

Coleridge, the poet, described written expression very succinctly when he said, 'Prose consists of the right words in the right order', and this simple definition gets right to the heart of the matter. If the self-expressionist wishes to pass on his ideas to other people (and presumably that is why he utters them) he must present them in a form acceptable to the majority. This is why it is necessary not only to spell in a conventional way but also to compose sentences which are conventionally constructed and do not offend the reader by their incomprehensibility. The right words must be in the right order.

The advocates of self-expression in infant and junior schools have a strange belief that writing is made up of two separate factors—ideas and mechanical accuracy. The former factor is highly esteemed and the latter regarded as pedestrian and unimportant. Over and over again, one has heard from lecturers, inspectors and advisers in education that children must be urged to express themselves freely and copiously, and that they must on no account be discouraged from pouring out their ideas by an inhibiting insistence on correct spelling and grammatical accuracy. 'Just let them write!' we are told.

It seems that this romantic notion is based on the false conception that poets and creative writers exude their ideas in a flood of words unrestrained by conventional sentence construction, and that if they had to bother about spelling or syntax they would lose their inspiration. This is far from the truth. The words of a language are, as it were, the tools of the writer, who has to recognise their form and grammatical function, and with them fashion phrases and sentences which can be easily understood by his readers and will convey to them the ideas which he has in mind.

The belief that little children have a store of exciting ideas which they are bursting to communicate is not borne out by experience. Ideas are very hard to come by, as any writer knows. Wordsworth, for example, did not sit down by Grasmere with pencil and paper and pour out his 'inspired' thoughts about the daffodils. The idea of the poem was secondhand, and was suggested by an entry in the journal of his sister Dorothy. It was not written at one attempt, but took several years for completion, and actually contained two lines written by the poet's wife. Similarly, Goleridge's oft-quoted lines, 'In Xanadu did Kubla Khan a stately pleasure-dome decree' are very similar to lines in *Purchas his Pilgrimage*, an old travel-book he had been reading before he sat down to write. These two are not by any means the only great poets and writers who have been glad to borrow ideas. Really original ones are scarce commodities. They seldom gush forth in a flood of inspiration. 'Genius,' in Thomas Edison's words, 'is one per cent inspiration and ninety-nine per cent perspiration.'

It is therefore strange that educationists should advise teachers of young children to let them write freely without the restraint of mechanical accuracy. Any experienced teacher knows that children's ideas are limited by their short and narrow experience of life. They cannot be expected to have much to say, and therefore it is better to give them the rudiments of writing-skill and then help them by suggesting ideas and topics about which they can express themselves reasonably accurately. There is no point in telling them to express themselves freely when they have few ideas to write about, and little writing expertise. Free or 'creative' writing, as it is now pompously called, can lead only to a formless rigmarole, offensive in its basic inaccuracy, unless the children who are writing it have been given some elementary grounding in putting the words of their native tongue together in readable sentence form.

This view was put forward in the Ministry's publication *Language*, published in 1954, where it stated, 'A generous measure of tolerance has been recommended towards spelling, and even towards punctuation, in the written composition of very young children, but even children of eight or nine ought not be be left unaware that writing is a craft, and that something more is expected, even at this age, than just a shapeless transcription of memories and impressions not perfectly formulated, even in the imagination.' During the past decade, however, this sound advice has been ignored, and free creative writing has swept the board. Spelling is out; punctuation is out; grammar is out and the little child is applauded while he tries to put on paper a string of ill-written words which, in the case of the average and below-average child, are often as incoherent as the gibberish of an ape.

But what of the more intelligent children? How have they fared in the new creative writing era? Some of the examples of written work which appear in junior school magazines show creative writing at its best, but nevertheless, many teachers think that for the majority of pupils there has been a definite falling-off in the presentation in readable language of the ideas which children seek to express. Justification for teachers' doubts about the creative writing method can be found in the complaints of university lecturers concerning the low standards of written English achieved by many undergraduates, who are, in intellectual ability, from the top 5 per cent of the population. A 'Use of English' paper has been introduced by some of the examination boards, specifically to ensure that would-be entrants to university can write their mother tongue with a certain minimum acceptable standard, but that such a paper should be considered necessary can only be construed as a reflection on the way written English is being taught in the schools.

Other criticisms of the standards achieved by secondary school children are from time to time published in the reports on the examination for the General Certificate of Education. In a recent report on English Language at Ordinary Level for one of the boards, it states that while in the last few years the work from schools has shown a willingness to use the candidate's own experience as interesting material for composition, there has been a steady decline in all the mechanical aspects of writing, such as spelling, punctuation and paragraphing. In other words, encouragement in free-writing has led to inaccurate expression. It is further stated that this decline may well arise from the same causes as the greater confidence in expression, namely, that the effects of newer teaching methods in the earlier stages of education may be percolating to the fifth and sixth forms of our secondary schools. The examiner notes that whereas at one time it was the poorer candidate who confused 'there' and 'their', and who did not know the difference between the use of a full stop and that of a comma, these elementary errors are becoming more widespread, until now quite able candidates who write intelligently, habitually commit these blunders. Mistakes that used to be rare, such as the confusion of 'no' and 'know', 'must of' for 'must have', 'by' instead of 'buy' are now endemic. The examiner concludes from these dismal errors that many pupils are brought up without any respect for correctness. They will spell a word like 'woollen' in three different ways in as many lines, and sometimes examiners find that candidate after candidate is totally ignorant of the use of the comma and the apostrophe. The final comment makes sobering reading for creative writing enthusiasts, 'It is difficult to understand how so many pupils can exhibit such elementary errors.'

It would have been reasonable to suppose that in this grand new scientific and technological age the necessity for clear, concise and accurate English would have been greater than in the past. With the advent of time-saving machines like computers, which deal so quickly and effectively with the technical data fed into them, it would have been understandable that insistence on a high standard of written communication between the people engaged on this type of work would be necessary. One would have thought that more scientific thinking would have necessitated a corresponding exactness of expression. It is therefore most surprising to read in the G.C.E. English examiner's report evidence that scientific progress does not necessarily result in more precise written work in schools. This is what is said on the subject, 'The haste apparent in much of the work leads to the use of colloquialisms and clichés, to ill-formed sentences strung together with "ands" and "thens" to the inclusion of much triviality that could profitably be pruned. Most candidates show that they have something to say that is worth saying, but they have not mastered the technique of expressing their ideas clearly and forcefully.'

That there should be this criticism of the writing of sixteen-year-old children who are in the top 25 per cent of the population is surely an indictment of the teaching methods which produce such loose expression. The frequency of 'ands' and 'thens' noted starts at the very beginning of a child's written work, when he is urged to write freely without paying attention to punctuation and correct sentence construction. If teachers are too sensitive or perhaps too lazy to draw children's attention to the inadequacy of their long rambling written statements, and are hesitant to indicate with the red pencil the defects in construction, then such errors are bound to persist even to the higher stages of education.

It is a pity that those who advise teachers in training and in the actual classroom should promulgate the thesis that free unrestrained writing is likely to produce better and more exciting ideas than written composition soundly based on a knowledge of punctuation and the rules of syntax. There is no evidence at all that thrilling ideas and good grammatical construction are incompatible. Indeed, there is ground for thinking that children who can write accurate English are much better able, and more likely, to produce ideas which show feeling and sensitivity. The ability to write well and easily enhances the prospect of vivid and lively expression.

This little poem was written by a boy of eight in a school where formal training in English expression begins in the first year of school life.

> In our garden stands an oak,
> And beneath—a baby oak.

> *The great big oak*
> *Often frowns down at our house,*
> *As if to say,*
> *'Now you stay away from my baby and me.'*
>
> R. Cossey

This little boy has a complete command of words, and uses them simply and accurately to express his sensitive idea of the father oak keeping guard over his baby. Is not this a good example of how early facility with words can heighten poetical feeling? Is it not better to write restrainedly and accurately than to be profuse but imprecise?

As a contrast, here is a piece of writing taken from a G.C.E. English script which was marked in 1969, 'Irriterbul dad cliped peets eerol hes allways up to all posiable mischiff amanagebel.'

It would be an interesting exercise to choose suitable adjectives other than 'free, unrestrained and copious' to describe such writing as this!

10

THE NEW MATHS CULT

Fashions in education are almost as frequent and bewildering as those in women's clothes. Teachers have hardly become used to the joys of printing with tree-bark when some adviser urges them to have a go at soap-sculpture, dough-modelling or painting with flower-sap. It is quite a job to keep up with all the new trends, but if a teacher is seriously thinking about promotion, then he must at least dabble in all of them. Craft subjects, of course, are prone to frequent innovation, but until ten years ago there was one subject on the time-table, Arithmetic, which was being taken on much the same lines as it was forty or fifty years before. Arithmetic is based on the immutable laws of number, and but for making a few mild excursions into unreality, such as Mathematics through Rabbit-keeping, and Counting on Bingo-cards, teachers have been resistant to changes in this subject.

In 1957, however, something happened which caused a revolution in the teaching of arithmetic in the schools. In that year the Russians, to the great chagrin of the Americans, put their first Sputnik into orbit, and the scientists and mathematicians of the West quickly went into a huddle to try to find how this formerly backward people had acquired the technological expertise to achieve this miracle. Rightly or wrongly, the blame for Russian superiority in the field of space-exploration was placed on the alleged out-of-date teaching of maths and science in our schools. If we had a new approach to these subjects we might ultimately catch up with the Russians. This might seem an over-simplification of what actually did take place with regard to new maths teaching, but certainly since the date of the first Sputnik's launching, a great change has taken place in English schools. Whereas up to Sputnik-time, Arithmetic had been the one solid and constant work-period in the curriculum, from now on this bastion of traditional formal method was to be handed over to the progressivists. Dr. Geoffrey Matthews, who became organiser of the Nuffield Project, summed up this transformation very neatly when he said, 'Up went the Sputnik, and down came the mathematicians saying we must do sets and be saved!'

What is this new maths which we hear so much about, and how does it differ from traditional 'sums'? It would be quite wrong to think that it is a new subject devised by some twentieth-century Newton or Descartes. It is rather a fresh presentation of traditional mathematical material with the addition of some new concepts, and a new terminology to explain and clarify the fresh thinking involved.

It is claimed that the pages and pages of sums which were set to children to make them familiar with the British system of weights and measures, the coinage and the four rules in number are not so necessary as they once were, because nowadays computers and calculating machines can do the most intricate calculations at lightning speed. We are no longer trying to educate working-class children to be clerks in offices or shop assistants who can give accurate change. We should be educating them for the space age, so mathematics must be given a new up-to-date slant. In the preamble to the Nuffield Mathematics Project publica-

WHY TOMMY ISN'T LEARNING

tion, *I Do, and I Understand*, it states why it is necessary to have a new modern maths. It argues that there is no longer any need for what is termed 'Victorian Arithmetic', which was something used by counting-house clerks who 'kept their ledgers meticulously, wrote in beautiful copperplate, neatly underlined their immaculate figures and whose calculations were always accurate.' It would seem that these paragons of the old Victorian elementary system, who were no doubt nourished on a diet of compulsory table-learning, pages and pages of formalised sums in the four rules and cane-motivated daily practice in mental arithmetic, become unnecessary in the increased tempo of modern life. Twentieth-century children need a new type of teaching in mathematics which prepares them for the age of automation. In this age, to quote the Nuffield pamphlet, 'There will be less need for people who can perform computations speedily and accurately, and more need for people who can assess situations and formulate and solve problems.'

What this last grandiloquent statement means is not entirely clear, but it would seem that having got rid of those neat, meticulously accurate counting-house clerks, we must train our children not to bother about such mundane, pedestrian tasks as table-learning and careful computation, but get them out into the playground, the fields, the woods and the wide open spaces, where, as any teacher knows, full scope can be given to forty lively little children to assess many diverse and wholly unpredictable situations. Moreover, to be slightly cynical, the teacher by initiating this splendid, adventurous approach to mathematics will no doubt have formulated, and it is to be hoped, solved many problems strictly outside the realm of the subject.

According to the Nuffield Mathematics Projectionists, it appears 'the time may now be ripe for the emancipation of arithmetic and for it to take its rightful place in the wider field of mathematics. It may even be that mathematics itself should be given a roving commission within the new world of primary education'. This grand-sounding advice about emancipation and roving commissions has had a revolutionary effect upon most primary schools in this country. It is a rare sight indeed today to find a class of children quietly working at desks during the arithmetic period occupied in doing formal sums. On entering a modern primary school one is struck by the absence of the formality which characterised the old elementary schools. Gone are the orderly rows of desks with children silently sitting in serried ranks while teacher expounds some arithmetical process. Gone is the repetitious sing-song of the chanted multiplication tables. Instead, one finds the jolly bustle of happy little children actively engaged in many diverse occupations. Here is a group said to be making a histogram concerning the personal data of their classmates—sizes of shoes, heights, weights and waist measurements—(and what a row they are making!); here another group claims to be plotting a graph showing the number of children with blonde, brunette, red and mouse-coloured hair; here some boys and girls are noisily weighing-out the ingredients for a cake; here some more seem to be making a lovely mess with buckets of water, but are actually programmed to be measuring their capacity, while from outside can be heard the joyful din of yet another group finding out the length and width of the playground with a trundle-wheel. These children have, it is claimed, been released from the bondage of having to do sums and learn tables—they are allegedly learning by personal experience. An observant onlooker, however, might ask if the diversity of occupations does not in fact militate against an ordered sequence of learning being followed, and he might further question if this happy hullabaloo were really conducive to the encouragement of logical thought.

In this new mathematical situation, the teacher's role is to move about among the children unobtrusively helping and advising like a benevolent big brother. However, one must not think that the children are always engaged upon such 'active' occupations as I have described above. There are occasions, of course, when they must be given some insight into the functions and properties of number, but even at these times there is no passive dependence upon formal bookwork. Keeping pace with the development of the new maths, educational suppliers have released on to the market dozens of practical aids to the understanding of the subject. In addition to trundle-wheels, weighing machines, capacity containers, clinometers and measuring-tapes, a whole variety of wooden and plastic rods and blocks have poured into the schools. Two of the notable best-sellers of the aids to mathematical understanding are the Cuisenaire rods and Dienes blocks, which are ingenious devices for helping children to understand mathematical concepts and relationships.

Without questioning the efficacy of all these practical aids to learning, it must be said that there is a very real danger of teachers placing too great emphasis on their use because they are fashionable and 'trendy'. Children should also be made aware that 'discovery' can be made from books as well as from material things, and that if they are ever to succeed in mathematics, sooner or later they must get down to some quiet thinking away from the noisy hurly and burly of the 'activity' classroom.

There is, moreover, one very great snag in the wholesale adoption by teachers of these wonderful new aids to maths teaching. In this new presentation of maths it is considered absolutely essential that an order of conceptual learning must be followed, and at no point in the learning sequence should any major principle or concept be presented to children which assumes other concepts not fully understood. You simply cannot use these intricately devised helps to learning without understanding the principles which underlie them. They are not tools for the amateur, and in the hands of teachers who have not been trained in their mystery, they can do more harm than good. The activity principle of learning has long been recognised in primary schools, but can the teacher be certain that every activity is purposeful, unless he himself is trained to be fully conversant with all the learning processes which he is using? Dr. Douglas Pidgeon, the Deputy Director of the National Foundation for Educational Research, who is an advocate of the new methods, issues a warning note when he says, 'Activity without purpose may in fact be harmful, for it is possible that the wrong kind of learning will take place. It is important therefore that the purpose of any learning task presented to a pupil must be fully understood by the teacher. This is not always the case unfortunately; many teachers using the Dienes approach to mathematics learning are unaware of many of the concepts they are presumably expecting their pupils to learn.'

Here is the core of the argument about the validity and worth of the new modern maths. Are the teachers in the average primary school fitted by ability and training to undertake the rethinking and reorganisation implicit in the transformation of Victorian 'Rithmetic into twentieth-century new-style mathematics? And if they are not, would it not be better for the children in their charge to be taught under the traditional 'tables and sums' system which brought such good results in the past? One of Her Majesty's staff Inspectors issued some cautionary words recently in the Ministry publication *Trends in Education*. This is what he said under the title, 'Modern Maths Reconsidered'. 'Too many innovations for the ordinary teacher have been introduced and he has been expected to change content at too great a pace. It is better to teach what one knows and has found to be of value than to fall a victim to "modernisation" and teach badly what is unfamiliar and of doubtful value. Already reformers have realised that they have neglected too much traditional algebra and arithmetic. All modern courses contain traditional material, but there are too many which contain so much new material that everything, new and old, is treated in too slight a fashion. Mathematics for the abler half of our school population requires thoroughness, the learning of techniques, a proper challenge in problem-solving, and a firmer grasp of systematically developed areas of knowledge than can come from that *fluttering over the surface* which characterises so many of today's courses. It is right to make some changes, particularly in methods, in the hope that they will be improvements. It is wrong to make wholesale changes in the belief that experiment has shown that they are necessary to achieve good and reasonable aims.' It is this 'fluttering over the surface' alluded to in the inspector's comment which causes concern to many experienced heads and assistant teachers who were trained in the disciplines of the traditional methods of arithmetic teaching. The merit of 'Victorian arithmetic' was that it was a no-nonsense down-to-earth subject. It was based on the hard facts of number, and it dealt in measurable concrete quantities like gallons of beer, tons of coal and yards of linoleum. Where children were 'doing sums' they were carrying out useful calculations that came within the ambit of their daily experience, and although critics of this kind of arithmetic always sneeringly cite the uselessness of doing problems about hot and cold taps filling baths while waste-pipes empty them, this type of question is at least based on understandable experience, and moreover, contains some fundamental reasoning principles. In any case, can the new mathematicians say that their sets, tessellations, curve-stitching, bar-charts and symmetry are more related to life than the bath-tap problem? No, I think that on relevance to real-life situations, Victorian arithmetic wins hands-down with the new maths.

For teachers of long experience, standards of skill in computation and manipulation of number are more important than dabbling in a new mathematics which seems too theoretical for the great majority of school-children. Teachers from an older generation remember that arithmetic text-books of forty years ago were, age for age, much more difficult and demanding than those of today. Indeed, children of today brought up on the rather tenuous ideas of the new maths, would find much of the solid mechanical and problem work contained in the arithmetic syllabuses of former years far too exacting. Advocates of the new maths often criticise the old arithmetics for containing only long cumbersome examples of mechanical calculations, but this is far from the case. In addition to the rows and rows of set sums, these text-books contained many problems and much geometry and algebra.

In Chapter 4, I showed that a much higher standard of arithmetic was expected from a child taking an eleven-plus examination in 1924 than was expected thirty-five years later from a student entrant taking maths in a women's training college. It could be argued that the eleven-plus paper which I showed was set to find clever grammar school entrants, and was therefore more difficult than the general run of arithmetic expected of eleven-year-olds at that time. However, to show what average children of twelve were expected to do forty years ago, I give below five examples taken from a Standard Six Arithmetic of that period. (Mc-Dougall's *Suggestive Arithmetics*, Edinburgh). These are from a page of miscellaneous examples set as revision of the typical year's course:

(i) Find the rate of profit obtained by selling for £27 10s. a piano that cost £20; and find also at what it should have been sold to gain 40 per cent.

(ii) Two parallelograms have equal bases 5 ft. 6 in. long. If the area of one is $13\frac{3}{4}$ sq. ft. and of the other $17\frac{7}{8}$ sq. ft., find their respective altitudes.

(iii) If 20 sq. in. be taken as equal to 129 sq. centimetres, express a square yard as a decimal of a sq. metre correct to 3 places.

(iv) Express in kilogrammes the weight of a kilometre of wire, 25 centimetres of which weigh 41 decigrammes.

(v) I received £275 18s. $1\frac{1}{2}d.$ in payment of principal and interest of a sum lent for 4 months at $3\frac{3}{4}\%$. How much was lent?

Such examples as these are as difficult as those set to sixteen-year-old G.C.E. candidates today, and yet they were the daily fare of average 12–13-year-olds forty years ago. Here are three examples from a G.C.E. Mathematics paper set this year:

(i) The sum of £16 amounts to £16 14s. in 15 months at simple interest. Calculate the rate per cent.

(ii) A car travels 15⅖ miles in 14⅔ minutes. Calculate its speed in miles per hour.

(iii) As a result of a 4% increase in price, a certain car now costs £780. Calculate the price of the car before the increase.

In comparing the two sets of examples, it should be noted that the former is the typical work asked of an average 12–13-year-old in 1929, but the latter is that expected of 16-year-old G.C.E. candidates, who are in the top 30 per cent of the school population in 1969. This comparison would seem to indicate that in arithmetical attainment children of forty years ago were, age for age, superior to those of today, and certainly standards of work in school text-books for average children have declined in those years, as an examination of the different series of arithmetics reveals. Many arithmetic text-books have had to be revised to adjust to this decline, and some of the more difficult ones have gone off the market. It will doubtless be argued by advocates of the new modern maths that while children of today may not have the ability to calculate as quickly and accurately as those of three or four decades ago, they have a better understanding of mathematical concepts. It would be hard to prove this, but in my view 'the thoroughness, the learning of techniques, the challenge of problem-solving and the firmer grasp of systematically developed areas of knowledge', which Mr. Lyness mentioned, are better inculcated by traditional arithmetic than by a dabbling in the pretentious theory of the modern maths. Of all subjects on the time-table, mathematics should be securely based on a firm structure of knowledge and intellectual skills acquired through systematic teaching. 'Fluttering over the surface' of the new mathematics, as is happening in so many primary schools, is unsatisfactory for the teacher and utterly disastrous for the taught.

11

THE FALLACY OF 'LEARNING BY STEALTH'

It was stated in Chapter 6 that the falling-off in the standards of achievement in the basic subjects of the curriculum began when the Report of the Consultative Committee urged that 'the curriculum is to be thought of in terms of activity and experience, rather than of knowledge to be acquired and facts to be stored'. This rather loose expression has led to some very loose thinking, and its effects upon school method have been disastrous. Now a curriculum is a course of study, and how you can follow one without first making up your mind what it is you want to teach is difficult to understand. There must be a definable body of knowledge in all subjects, and this will contain the facts which the children have to learn. All knowledge consists of facts, and a step-by-step assimilation of those facts which are deemed desirable is the basis of learning. There is no escape from this. Activity and experience are not enough.

Now the originators of the Elementary System of Education in England knew about the value of facts, and they knew that the little boys and girls whom they had compelled to come to school would not have acquired many of consequence prior to their school-entry. These children, if you like, were virgin soil waiting for the seeds of knowledge to be sown. The classes were huge; many of the children were unwilling participators in the learning process; school life was short, and so the method of teaching had to be quick and efficient. It was quite natural therefore that the inculcation of the facts of a particular course of study was the prime aim of the teacher. It had been noted that children quickly forget facts, and that frequent repetition is the best aid to memory. It is thus not surprising that in learning to read, children were trained in the sounds which the letters of the alphabet make. By constant repetition they quickly became familiar with them and soon learnt to read. Similarly, in arithmetic they learnt the number bonds—4 + 5, 7 + 2, 6 + 3—and in time the multiplication tables which they could reel off automatically at the teacher's bidding. Such subjects as history and geography were taken by teachers in as interesting a manner as the limited visual aids of those days allowed, but ultimately the facts of these subjects had to be committed to memory, just like the facts of reading and arithmetic.

Critics of the elementary system often jibe at the repetitious nature of the learning, and sly sneers about memorising the names and dates of the kings and queens of England in history and the capes and bays of Britain in geography are usually part of that criticism. It is suggested that teachers in those 'bad old days' did little else but compel their pupils to learn things by rote. This, however, is a misrepresentation of what went on in most schools at that time. Things were not by any means as dull as the detractors of the system maintain. Here is an entry from my old school log book, September 13th, 1901: 'Miss Butler and Miss de la Coze took their classes, Standards 1 and 2, to Cooper's Hill and gave the children a geography lesson with the view before them.' School visits such as these were not by any means uncommon in those days, and journeys into the Great Park to study nature, and to the College to see the picture gallery were part of the education provided, but these mildly exciting excursions were not allowed to divert teachers or children from the main task of learning—the assimilation of the necessary facts.

It must be stated here quite plainly that the inculcation of facts with large classes is very hard and unremitting toil. It is not jolly and exciting and rewarding. It is demanding, and is only effective with teachers who have good class control. This explains why the relaxation of the strict discipline which was the foundation of the didactic method of teaching was not, of course, unwelcome in some quarters. Those who were not effective teachers under the system were no doubt glad that now knowledge need no longer be acquired nor facts stored. Children would be able, as Rousseau desired, to teach themselves by experience. It would be guidance rather than instruction, and how much less exhausting it is to watch children discovering things for themselves than to have to drive facts home! It is true, however, that although the encouragement to teachers to think in terms of activity and experience rather than about knowledge and facts was given by the Ministry of Education as long ago as 1931, many of them refused to change from their formal methods, and continued with their old-fashioned didactic mode of teaching.

Since the last war, however, there has been great pressure from inspectors, college lecturers, psychologists and amateur educators of all kinds to spread the doctrine of discovery methods, and to promote an education which is child-centred in the best Dewey tradition. The infant schools, which had been greatly influenced by Margaret McMillan's nursery school theories, were quick to abandon didactic methods, and adopted the Playway with enthusiasm, so that it would be true to say today that no infant teacher forces facts on a child, but waits patiently for him to discover them for himself. This, of course, means a prolongation of the learning period, because clearly it must take longer to find things out by trial and error than to be directly instructed in those same facts by a teacher. However, this does not disturb the progressive educationist. He believes with Piaget that a child must be allowed to do his own learning. This is known as an 'inherent motivation process' as opposed to the 'imposed motivation' which characterises the didactic method of teaching. Piaget puts it thus: 'The teacher must provide the instruments which the children can use to decide for themselves.' And then he makes this odd assertion: 'A ready-made truth is only a half-truth.' In other words, a teacher must not say, 'This is so.' but must provide a situation for the child to discover the truth for himself.

This advice is really an extension of the method advocated by Rousseau two hundred years ago. In writing of the best way to teach his Emile, he said: 'Surround him with all the lessons you would have him learn without awaking his suspicions.' What a devious, dishonest, underhand way to set about the education of children! Yet this statement is the basis for the underlying principle of modern teaching method. Children must not be inculcated with facts in an open and direct manner. They must be enticed and cajoled into discovering things for themselves by the provision of situations where it is believed knowledge may lie. Blissfully unaware of what is happening to them, the children are literally trapped into learning by their scheming teachers.

This manner of educating, which has been rightly if cynically called 'learning by stealth', is by its nature a slower method than the didactic one, and has in my view been more responsible than anything else for the decline in standards of achievement which I think has taken place. Such a method in the hands of dedicated, competent teachers, trained in the principles behind it, might have a place in our system of education for certain types of children, but for the average run-of-the-mill teacher and child it is far preferable to stick to the tried, traditional approach. Unfortunately, in order to please inspectors and obtain promotion, many teachers have jumped on the progressive bandwagon and profess to be teaching by methods in which they are only really competent to dabble. This has led to the multitude of stunts and gimmicks which have delighted and deceived inspectors over the past three or four decades. Publishers and educational suppliers have naturally cashed-in on the plausible attractiveness of the new ideas, and schools have been filled with aids and apparatus whose practical value can best be gauged by the transience of their usefulness. There is one ironic aspect of this use of gimmicks in the classroom. Because the unusual and the bizarre make exciting news, much more attention is paid by the Press and B.B.C. to the progressive stunts which appear in the classroom from time to time than to the ordinary humdrum practice of the traditional formal style of teaching. Such topics as 'Bingo Brightens Backward Boys', 'Dartboard Maths' or 'Geography in the Supermarket' are thrilling things to report even though they may not be very effective learning aids for the children engaged in these news-making pursuits.

It is these children, like Tommy the retarded reader,

who are the chief sufferers from the method of teaching by stealth. Tommy is an average little boy who failed to learn to read in the infants' school, because the association of words with pictures on flash-cards did not provide the basic understanding that letters are intended to indicate sounds. What he needed was some good old-fashioned drill in phonics until his response to letter-sounds was automatic. 'How deadly dull and frustrating!' say the progressives. 'How much jollier for the child to learn by pictorial association, even if it does take a little longer!' Now drill in letter-sounds can be a bit tedious for both teacher and taught, but surely training in hard work and concentration is part of a teacher's task. When Tommy has learnt to read through memorising the letter-sounds, the pleasure and sense of achievement at being able to 'crack the code' instead of watching the pictures will more then compensate for any tedium involved in the learning process.

Tommy's inability to read at seven is a great handicap and makes all learning from that point difficult and disagreeable. He has suffered with many others of the same age from a form of schooling which is diffuse and imprecise. Little children need definite, firm and direct instruction in the matters which it is proposed to teach them. They dislike vagueness and delight in repetitive tasks. They are at that age ready to memorise facts and take great pleasure in imitation, so that they can easily be led to copy any learning material presented to them directly and purposefully. They are waiting to be told what to do, so to ask them to discover things for themselves is too vague and insubstantial a request. They like to know where they are going, and they want to be shown the way.

In the junior school, Tommy, handicapped by his

poor reading, has little to gain from learning by stealth. He cannot even read the written suggestions laboriously prepared by his teacher to involve him in the learning situation. Neither can he make notes about what he is attempting to do while discovering, because he cannot write. For such children as Tommy, and there are many of them today, the idea of learning by discovery methods is ludicrous. They need more than anything to be taught how to read, and all the energies of the teachers in the junior school should be directed to that end. Hand in hand with systematic teaching in reading should go formal practice in writing the words and sentences which can be read. System and formality are in fact essentials in the learning process. While it might be possible to teach a very small group of highly intelligent children to learn by discovery methods, as is done in some private boarding-schools, the state schools with their huge classes and large proportion of average and below average pupils are quite unsuitable for such practices. Learning at junior level must be from prepared material which has been structured in easily understood steps. Each step or stage should be part of a graduated scheme, so that the child as well as the teacher can see the progress that is being made, and repetition and revision of the knowledge acquired should be made regularly at every stage. There may be some value in allowing the first few months in the infants' school to be a time for practising informal play techniques, but if these are prolonged, then the child will be slow to come to grips with the difficulties of real learning. He will have become so used to playing that he will be loath to make the effort necessary for purposeful learning.

Tommy, and the many other children in our schools

of similar mental ability and personal characteristics, need, above all things, a strong lead from their teachers. To expect 'inherent motivation' in their approach to school work is just sentimental wishful thinking. Tommy is no more industrious and conscientious than the thousands of other little boys and girls of his age. Like them, he is inclined to be idle and seek the easy way out; like them, he is spasmodic in his efforts and easily diverted from the matter in hand; like them, he would sooner be playing football or watching television than doing school tasks. He is, however, much more astute than he is given credit for. He is not easily taken in by the blandishments of the progressive teacher, nor deceived by the elaborate artifices of the learning by stealth method. He is, in his worst moments, not above using the little Dienes blocks as classroom projectiles or borrowing a Cuisenaire rod or two for fishing floats. He is in fact the normal, lazy, naughty little boy who has been annoying and delighting us since the world began.

For him 'inherent motivation' is a fanciful conceit! He needs, above all, the 'imposed motivation' which comes from a quiet, orderly classroom, controlled by a firm but kindly teacher, who knows what she wants from her pupils and is determined to get it. There is a fundamental defect in the 'learning by stealth' method of educating children. It is the notion that by enticing children into learning you make them more amenable to the educative process, and that in making things easier for them, you necessarily make them happier. This is a foolish fallacy. If children are not trained in the early stages to undertake demanding tasks with cheerfulness they are not likely to develop into industrious, cheerful men and women. We should be teaching them from the first to tackle difficult things with enthusiasm, and training them to discover the feeling of achievement which only hard work can bring. You will never develop good future citizens by luring children to their lessons. They need vigorous persuasion, not an enervating enticement.

It is not surprising that those who advocate the method of 'learning by stealth' should have enlisted the aid of educational psychologists in condemning the traditional didactic mode of teaching. They claim that any firm direction of pupils in study is repressive and harmful to the ego, and that tests of knowledge and competition for places in class can cause neuroses which may adversely affect the child for the rest of his life, whereas the encouragement of creative self-expression so nourishes the child's subconscious that he develops naturally into a balanced adult free of frustration and inhibition. This Utopian theory would be far more convincing if there were any indication or evidence that it had been effective in practice. For all the supposed avoidance of psychological damage by not imposing simple discipline on younger children, how much lasting damage is done to them when they finally leave school unable to read and write with ease?

12

DISAPPEARING STANDARDS

British schools are probably subject to less interference in matters of organisation and curriculum than those of any European country, and British teachers are quite rightly jealous of their autonomy in the classroom. Under France's completely centralised system of education, it is said that the Minister of Education in Paris can say what the pupils in day schools in places as widely apart as Bordeaux, Brest and Besançon, would be engaged in studying at any given moment. This may be an exaggeration, but it is certainly true that in France, the nation of individualists, teachers are prepared to submit to more central control of curriculum and subject content than their counterparts in Britain.

British schools have not always been as free as they are today. When the Elementary System began, there was a strict code of rules for the conduct of schools, and yearly standards of achievement in the basic subjects were laid down for teachers' guidance. Even after the hated 'payment by results' system had gone, Inspectors from the Board of Education still came into the schools to test the pupils' performance in the basic subjects, and reports on these visits were based on their findings. Publishers' text-books for schools were geared to the expected attainments of the yearly age groups, and classes were officially called 'standards', where the seven-year-olds were classified as Standard One, and the thirteen-year-olds Standard Seven. There were not only text-books in reading, arithmetic and English specifically written for the seven standards but subjects like history, geography and nature-study also had their sets of seven graded volumes. It was a businesslike system for conducting schools, and ensured that everybody involved knew exactly what he was supposed to be doing. There were defined standards at which to aim, and for the certificated teacher, who was expected to teach classes of sixty children in the early nineteen hundreds, no other system would have been practicable or endurable. It produced a species of teacher whose approach may have been authoritarian, but whose efficiency at instructing large groups of children to defined standards was incontestable.

As classes have become smaller (fifty was the limit in 1924, and forty in 1945), there has been a general relaxation in the severe discipline so necessary for controlling sixty children, and teachers have adopted a less rigid approach to the problems of the classroom. The system of standards for the various age groups has gone, and children are supposed to be educated in accordance with their aptitude and ability. This means that the less able will not be expected to work at the same pace as those of high ability, and so individual development becomes the teacher's main preoccupation. When children are working at individual assignments or discovering things at their own pace it becomes quite impossible to set standards of achievement for the various age-groups. It is useless for Tommy's mother to complain at the school about his backwardness, for the reply will come quite pat from the teacher, 'Tommy is working at his own pace and to the full extent of his ability.' And who can quarrel with that?

With the end of stipulated standards for the different age-groups, the need for formal Ministry inspection of schools has lessened, and today the five hundred Her Majesty's Inspectors of Schools are little more than educational advisers. As there is no longer a reliable yardstick by which to judge the progress of children, tests of subject attainment are no longer set to pupils, and so there cannot be the same inducement to urge children on to definite standards of achievement. Moreover, the general adoption by teachers of activity methods makes it more and more difficult for visiting inspectors to judge fairly the merits of schools. Where classes of children are allegedly involved in finding out by discovery, each at his own pace, the traditional role of the Inspector has become outdated. His visits are now purely perfunctory. He can only smile benignly at what he sees, and spend more and more of his time in organising courses and reporting on the inadequacy of buildings.

Although standards in schools have, as we have seen, ceased to be clearly defined, there was until recently in the junior schools one remaining yardstick of achievement in the basic subjects—the selection examination for secondary schools. This exam, although taking different forms under different local authorities, did by setting tests in arithmetic, English and verbal reasoning act as a yearly academic hurdle for the eleven-year-olds in primary schools. It ensured that fourth-year junior classes had to be given specific instruction in certain arithmetical, English and reasoning skills, and in this respect it helped to maintain standards of attainment. The Plowden Report, as would be expected, is in favour of abolishing selection procedures, but it wisely foresees what this entails. This is what it says; 'with the ending of selection examinations, teachers and parents will need some yardstick of the progress of their children in relation to what is achieved elsewhere'. It then goes on to advocate the use of objective tests[1] in schools because their norms can be used as a basis of comparison.

We must applaud Plowden for seeing the snags in the abolition of eleven-plus testing, but it is the fashionable trend towards individual and active learning which the report heartily endorses, that is in my opinion the chief agent in the lowering of standards of achievement in schools. In the second Black Paper on education that great educationist, Professor Sir Cyril Burt, makes this alarming statement, 'Judged by tests applied and standardized in 1913–14, the average attainments in reading, spelling, mechanical and problem arithmetic are now appreciably lower than they were fifty years ago. The deterioration is most marked in English Composition. Here the vogue is all for "creativity". Bad spelling, bad grammar, and the crudest vulgarisms are no longer frowned upon, but freely tolerated. Instead of accuracy the teacher aims at self-expression; instead of clear and logical thought or precise description of facts, he—and still more often she—seeks to foster what is called "imagination".' In support of this statement, Sir Cyril refers his readers to an article by him in the *Journal of Educational Psychologists*, where he states his findings for the latest available data on the use of his standardised educational tests. Taking the norms for 1914 as 100·0, the latest figures are Accuracy

[1] 'Objective tests' are tests of achievement in which the element of subjective opinion has been eliminated. Several choices of response are given to a set test question, and the candidate has to pick the right one, e.g. Which of the words in the bracket is the same as the given word? ENOUGH: (few, much, sufficient, little, often, many). Such tests are usually strictly timed and contain 100 questions. They are convenient for standardising and for making comparisons. A 'NORM' is a standard determined by taking the average of the results of an objective test.

of Reading 95·4, Comprehension 99·3, Spelling 91·1, Mechanical Arithmetic 92·5, Problem Arithmetic 96·3. Sir Cyril states that it is the formal subjects like these that are likely to suffer by the adoption of informal methods. He then proceeds to lay the blame for the decline in standards on the new methods, saying, 'My own conclusion tallies with that of Professor Wiseman: "Much harm has been done by the uncritical and thoughtless adoption of progressive methods by teachers with little grasp of the basic philosophy behind them; for weak teachers such methods may be beyond their capacity; they are perhaps safer with the formal methods which they do understand."'

It is to be noted that Spelling, Mechanical Arithmetic and Reading show the worst declines from the 1914 norms. While such statistics as these may not mean much to a layman, they do surely indicate that there has been a definite deterioration in quality of achievement in these basic subjects of the school curriculum. Smaller classes, longer teacher training, more educational aids and better buildings surprisingly do not seem to have resulted in the expected higher standards which the period of fifty-five years since 1914 seems to have witnessed in medicine, engineering, science and most other spheres of human activity.

It would seem from the clear decline in standards revealed by the figures which Sir Cyril Burt quotes, that the absence of defined grades of attainment in the basic subjects, which goes with the adoption of informal methods in schools, is bound to have an adverse effect on British education. Without clearly defined aims and stated standards, conscientious teachers are bewildered because they have no systematic plan of school progress to which they can devote their energies, while the lazy and incompetent ones shelter in the shadowy vagueness of the learning by experience system.

Now that informal activity methods are becoming generally acceptable in British schools, what can be done to ensure that standards in the basic subjects do not decline still further? The Plowden Committee thinks that there should be recurring national surveys of attainment in reading and mathematics, but while this is a belated step in the right direction, there is little point in this recommendation unless the teachers in the schools have been given definite standards of attainment at which to aim. In my view we should establish overall national standards which children should be trained to reach at different stages. One obvious stage is at the transfer age from infant or first school to junior or middle school. Another stage would be at the transfer age of eleven or twelve to the secondary or comprehensive school.

Now it will probably be argued that it is impossible to lay down standards of achievement for all schools, because the quality of pupils varies from district to district, and the various methods of teaching in vogue produce diverse capabilities in pupils which are not measurable by any system of standardised tests. This is a plausible argument, but it does not absolve the local authorities and the Ministry from their duty to ensure that a reasonable standard of literacy and arithmetical/mathematical attainment shall have been achieved at certain stages of child development. We know that children differ widely in natural ability and environmental background, but it should not be beyond the wit of teachers to get together and decide just what ought to be expected of average children at the two transfer stages mentioned above. There has been in existence since 1964 an independent body with a majority of teacher members which was set up specifically to survey curriculum and examinations. This Schools Council, as it is called, would be just the organisation capable of considering and stating some simple achievement standards for the two vital transfer stages.

Having laid down some basic standards for schools, it would be necessary to have recurring tests as recommended by Plowden. These should be on a national scale, and would cover reading, written English and mathematics. It might be acceptable to teachers to agree to a National Test Day for the 10–11-year age group, on a specified date in the summer term. The tests could be marked by the teachers in their own schools on the following day, which would be declared a school holiday. The results of these tests would not be published outside the school, but would be filed for future reference. They would be passed on to the heads of secondary or comprehensive schools, where they would be invaluable for the yearly arrangement of intake forms. From the data obtained by the tests the Ministry would have valid norms for future comparisons.

Doubtless some heads would regard what I have suggested as an interference with their freedom to run their schools as they wished. There is, however, no suggestion that they should change their methods of teaching or organisation. Whatever methods they use, however, they should be prepared to submit to a test of their effectiveness. Parents have a right to know that their children are being taught to certain attainable levels, and whether they live in Bootle or Bournemouth, Aberystwyth or Ashby de la Zouch, they need assurance that the schools in those towns have similar aims and common standards of attainment.

13

WHAT'S WRONG WITH TEACHER TRAINING

When considering the standards of work of the children in the schools, and devising ways of keeping those standards at a satisfactory level, it is, of course, vitally necessary to assess the calibre of the teachers in the classroom. It is necessary also to give some close thought to the institutions responsible for the training of those teachers.

Recently, the colleges of education have come under fire from several quarters. In an earlier chapter mention was made of the critical resolution which was almost unanimously passed by delegates of the 1969 conference of the National Association of Head Teachers. This asserted that an investigation was needed into the output of teachers inadequately prepared in fundamental teaching skills, and demanded the setting up of a working committee to examine the whole question of teacher training. In 1964 a conference of the heads of London's comprehensive schools produced a report on teacher training which complained that the three-year training course was not turning out people competent enough in the subjects they had to teach, nor in the methods of teaching them. The following comments from this report indicate the headteachers' misgivings about the quality of teacher training. 'Students now get their certificates and diplomas when they are one year older; they come into our schools to that degree less immature and naïve. But their personal education is often surprisingly shallow. The standard of their studies often seems to recede from that they achieved in the sixth forms of their schools. Their programme in the first two years still appears to be unduly fragmented by teaching practices and by the formal education courses. In short, we felt that the interval of three years between the departure of our sixth form pupils into training colleges and their return to us as probationary teachers might well be more imaginatively filled than it often is at present. Most of our conference assured us that in this view we were supported by a not inconsiderable body of opinion in the training colleges themselves.'

These strong criticisms from the people who have most right to complain—the consumers of the products of the colleges—received implied support from the members of the Plowden Committee, who at the end of their chapter on primary school teachers, recommended first of all, 'There should be a full enquiry into the system of training teachers.'

This dissatisfaction with the preparation of students for the ordeal of the classroom, has recently been emphasised in a more specific way by some comments in an interim report on a full-scale literacy survey carried out by the Inner London Education Authority. During the past two years, 32,000 eight-year-olds in London have had their reading skills tested and compared with national samples. Rather surprisingly, the Cockney kids, who have always been claimed to be inherently and environmentally quicker and more astute than their provincial counterparts, came out very badly on these tests. Put quite simply, the statistics in this report reveal that London's eight-year-olds are six months behind the national sample in reading attainment, and that there are proportionately twice as many 'poor' readers in the metropolis. One of the reasonable explanations for this reading backwardness is that London has a high proportion of immigrant children, but the report suggests too that the free programmes introduced in the infant departments may have some influence on reading standards. To quote, 'Some who teach infants may need help in injecting "precise" teaching into the free programme they have adopted.'

It may be asked: Who has been injecting *'imprecise'* notions of teaching reading and indeed of other subjects, into the teachers in London's schools? The answer to the query is implied in a further comment in this disturbing analysis of London's reading ills. Only one in eight of London's junior teachers has received specific training in reading techniques. No wonder that Mrs. Lena Townsend, the leader of the Inner London Education Authority, is to ask the Department of Education and Science for a full enquiry into teacher training.

Now it seems from the above evidence, that the poor old colleges of education are receiving a large proportion of blame for the malaise which is afflicting the body educational, but in fairness to those colleges, this body is suffering partly from the effects of too rapid and unrestricted growth. In order to cope with the raising of the school-leaving age to fifteen, and the voluntary staying-on of many more children to sixteen owing to greatly improved secondary school provision, there has been a sharp increase in the number of teachers required to staff the schools. Progressive reduction in the size of classes, and extension of training to three years, have further added to this problem, so that in order to maintain an adequate supply of teachers, the colleges of education have been strained to the limit of their resources. Since 1960 they have been engaged on an expansion programme which has more than doubled the number of places in the colleges.

When the novelist Kingsley Amis suggested that as the number of places in universities increased, the quality of the British degree might decline, and uttered his oft-quoted warning that 'More means worse', he was assailed as an 'élitist': his phrase could perhaps have been just as fairly applied to the greatly increased influx of entrants to the teaching profession. In an earlier chapter reference was made to the poor performance in spelling achieved by the students of one training college, and how the college authorities had tried to help them improve. Professor Brian Cox, who is Professor of English at Manchester University and joint-editor of *Black Paper Two*, was so appalled at the low quality of some students in training colleges that he stated in an article in the *Daily Telegraph*: 'It is quite usual to find students in their final year at Colleges of Education who cannot punctuate their sentences correctly and cannot spell simple words. Such incompetence is accompanied by incoherence in thought and expression. There are now many teachers in schools who might be called semi-literate.' At a press conference on the *Black Paper*, Professor Cox made the startling revelation that as an external examiner in English to twelve colleges of education under three universities—Leeds, Manchester and Exeter—at least 25 per cent of the examination papers out of many hundreds of scripts had been marked 'C' grade because of their low standard of literacy. In his view he had been passing teachers who should have failed, but as these students would have been passed by examiners for other colleges of education, he felt it would have been unfair not to do like-wise. He had, however, protested in report after report to the Universities Examinations Board about the unsatisfactory standard of students' written work.

Since making this statement, Professor Cox has with-drawn his services as external examiner to the twelve colleges of education, but his courageous protest about these semi-literate teacher students raises the question in most thoughtful people's minds, 'Has more meant worse in the case of training college entrants?' and a further question, 'Are five passes at ordinary general certificate level a high enough standard to ensure that we are admitting to colleges students who can emerge into the teaching profession as reasonable educated and cultured people?' It is true that recently many students applying for admission to college have secured one or two Advanced levels to offer in addition to their statutory minimum of five 'O' level passes, but the fact remains that five passes in a separate-subject examina-tion are not a sufficiently demanding standard as a basis for entry to a profession such as teaching. Until 1951, the entrance minimum to teaching was the School Certificate, which like other European leaving schools examinations today, had compulsory groups of subjects, from which English and five others had to be taken at a single sitting. The five other subjects had to include a science, a foreign language and mathematics. To obtain the school certificate, it was necessary to have passed in the full six subjects and fulfil the group conditions. You could not take one or two subjects at a time as is so often done today, and this did ensure that someone who had obtained the certificate had made the effort to achieve a good standard in a wide field of studies. There were no 'soft options', and this deterred the lazy and incompetent from trying to enter a profession like teaching.

The Plowden Report, while claiming that the general level of academic qualifications of students is satisfactory, admits there are aspects which cause disquiet. One of these is that a quarter of the men and two-fifths of the women entering college have not gained the 'minimum standard of numeracy' indicated by the possession of a pass at 'O' level in mathematics in the G.C.E. This would explain the desperately low standard of the Mathematics Grading Test set to women entrants to college which I quoted earlier. It would seem, moreover, that some students at least are not only semi-literate but 'semi-numerate' as well.

The colleges of education cannot be blamed for the low academic qualities of some of their students, because the standard of admission has been laid down by the Department of Education, but it would seem that this is not high enough. The low pass mark acceptable in the G.C.E. 'O' level in English does not make this examination a suitable criterion for selecting truly literate teachers—ones whose spoken and written English not only enables them to deal satisfactorily with the subjects they are teaching, but also inspires their pupils to higher standards of expression. An 'A' level pass in English should in my view be the minimum qualification for entry to college, and for those who are going to teach mathematics, 'A' level maths should be the established minimum.

Whatever the quality of their intake, the colleges have three years in which to train students to become competent teachers, and this time is spent about equally on academic and professional training. The two courses run concurrently, so that while students are increasing their knowledge of the subjects they have chosen, they are learning at the same time methods of passing this on to the children in the schools. In most colleges the proportion of time spent on practice teaching is stepped up from year to year. Thus in the first year, three weeks is the rule, in the second year four weeks and in the final year seven or eight weeks are spent in the actual classroom.

There is much criticism of college staff, in that they are out of touch with what goes on in the classroom. In the McNair Report of 1944, this complaint was underlined in the following statements, 'The core of the staff of any training institution must consist of men and women who not only have the requisite standing in their subjects but have proved themselves as teachers. The difficulty is to ensure that members of staff have recent and intimate experience of current school problems and practice. We should not be dealing faithfully with our subject, if we did not record that one of the criticisms levelled against the training colleges by some of the young teachers who gave us evidence, was that those who instructed and supervised them in the arts of teaching were not always themselves sufficiently acquainted with school conditions and practice.'

Since McNair, colleges have tried to ensure that their new staff are not only well qualified in their subjects but have also had some teaching experience. There is, however, still the feeling among many students and practising teachers that those who are telling the trainees what to do in class would probably have a job to carry out the instructions themselves. It is the age-old problem of the clash between theory and practice. One obvious way to ensure that college lecturers are not only purveyors of teaching methods, but also capable exponents of them, would be for them to continue to teach part-time in schools or else return to the classroom for a period every seven years. Such 'sabbatical' years would be more profitably spent than they sometimes are at present, in absences on theoretical courses in educational practice. This suggestion is not likely to be followed, however, because of almost certain opposition from the staff itself. As Dr. Koerner says in his book, *Reform in Education*, 'The fact must be faced that many people join a College staff, precisely to escape the rigours of teaching in the schools. One does find an occasional College staff member whose speciality is pedagogical methods, and who also continues to teach in schools, but it is rare. The vast majority do not even demonstrate their theories to their own student teachers in an actual classroom situation.' What a lamentable state of affairs!

What should we think of a master plumber who shunned demonstrating to his apprentices how to put a thread on a water-pipe or a washer on a tap? Yet most college lecturers would, I think, be reluctant to demonstrate the tricks of the trade which constitute the apprenticeship of teaching.

Yet of all the professions, teaching does need a period of try-out, of trial and error, for the young practitioner. To have read books by educational experts, or to have written papers on the theories of Rousseau, Froebel and Dewey, does not make one a satisfactory classroom practitioner. The proud title of Competent Teacher can be earned only through the ordeal of the classroom, and whether one teaches by the old-fashioned 'talk and chalk' formal method or through the freedom of activity and discovery, to achieve success one must first establish that mysterious rapport with children which only experience can bring. Children have to be controlled, whether by persuasion or gentle coercion. There is no escape from this, and college lecturers ought all to be successful teachers who can demonstrate in the classroom all the little tricks of gesture, of tone and of vigorous action which help to bring children to that responsive frame of mind which enables them to learn.

There has been criticism of the college course recently in a report prepared by the National Young Teacher Advisory Committee of the National Union of Teachers.[1] This report was based on questionnaires sent out to 560 young teachers, and covered among other things an assessment by them of twenty-six basic topics which it was judged were essential to a teacher training course. The young teachers were asked to say if these topics had been covered at college under four degrees of an efficiency rating—viz. Good, Adequate, Inadequate, Not taught. The replies given indicated that such matters as team teaching, integrated studies and teaching of immigrant children were all badly covered at colleges, and the teaching of that most important subject of the primary school curriculum—reading—was also badly neglected. The report says, 'The teaching of reading was rated as either not covered or inadequately dealt with by half of the primary respondents. This figure reflects a particularly crucial and apparently intransigent weakness in many college courses.'

What an indictment of the training college system is

[1] The National Union of Teachers has a Young Teacher Advisory Committee, which in 1969 conducted an enquiry into the efficacy of teacher training and issued a report from which I quote.

contained in these views of the ex-students of the colleges of education!

The young teachers make a practical suggestion to improve the deficiencies of the colleges with regard to practical teacher training and urge what they call 'a regular two-way dialogue between schools and those responsible for teacher education'. They suggest that there should be a system of school-based teacher-tutors who should aid and advise student-teachers, and they further urge that some means should be devised whereby there can be regular job-exchanges between skilled teachers and college lecturers.

If such revolutionary suggestions can be given practical application, and the teachers in the schools be given full responsibility for training students in the expertise of classroom control and day-to-day organisation, then the probationer teacher will commence his first job with more confidence and skill than he does at present.

The Plowden Report[1] agrees with the students that the colleges should have more contact with the schools, and suggests that in large schools graded posts carrying payment should be given to certain teachers who will take responsibility for supervising students and probationers. This is indeed a practical step in the right direction, and will, it is to be hoped, in time remove the scandal of fully trained teachers not having learnt at college how to teach such basic essentials as reading and other equally rudimentary scholastic skills.

[1] The Central Advisory Council for Education was asked by the Minister of Education in 1963 to consider the whole question of primary schooling and the transition to secondary education. This council issued its report in 1966. It is referred to as The Plowden Report because the chairman of the council was Lady Plowden.

14

CAJOLERY OR CONTROL

When Mr. Forster's Act of 1870 laid the foundations of the Elementary System of Education, it very properly stipulated what the curriculum of the schools should include. Although the main purpose of the Act was to teach the illiterate masses to read and write and calculate, these subjects, strangely enough, were placed second to morality and religion in order of precedence by the first School Board. Religious Knowledge in fact always appeared in early school time-tables as the first subject of the day, because the Victorians wanted their children, above all things, to be brought up on sound moral principles, for they believed with the Psalmist that 'the fear of the Lord is the beginning of wisdom'. In those days the schoolmaster's role was not confined to the direction of studies. He also had a magisterial function, and was expected not only to keep order in school but also to exercise a law-abiding influence on his pupils after the school day was over. He often punished children for minor misdemeanours committed in the evenings or school holidays, and parents cheerfully acquiesced in these punishments rather than see their offspring brought before the courts. A good and strict schoolmaster had a beneficial effect upon his locality, and was respected on this account.

Since the First World War there has been a gradual change in the outlook of the community to religion, and the imposition of any form of authority is frequently resented as an unjustifiable curtailment of the freedom of the individual. We have seen how this change of outlook has affected educational theory, and how the teachings of Rousseau, Froebel and Dewey have caused a revolution in the classroom. 'Imposed motivation' has given way to a freedom in school which would have appalled the Victorians, and a new leniency to child offences both in and out of school has, in my view, increased the figures for juvenile delinquency year after year. Between the years 1955 and 1965 the number of juveniles charged and proved guilty before the court went up from 11,289 to 18,212, an increase of 62 per cent, and this rise seems likely to continue. It is strange that the significance of the consistent rise in juvenile crime figures, being coincident with the adoption of 'free' methods in schools, has not been noted, and has not, moreover, caused a revulsion against the child-centred philosophy of education which could well have brought it about. A. S. Neill, Head of that most progressive of all schools, Summerhill, where the children have freedom to swear, call the teachers by their surnames and attend lessons only when they want to, has recently stated in his book, *Talking of Summerhill*, that if every child were reared in the Summerhill way juvenile crime would decrease enormously. He complains, 'The demand is still curing by authority and too often fear. One terrible result is that juvenile crime increases every year.' Neill does not admit that it is perhaps the relaxation of parental and school authority that has caused the steady soar in the figures of children's crime.

It seems to me, however, that the dramatic change in the relationship between teacher and pupil which has taken place in schools during the past thirty or forty years is as much as anything responsible for behavioural problems in school and home. Little children need the calm and security which only an orderly and quiet atmosphere can give. They need also the protective assurance of a teacher who through a benevolent authority will tell them what he expects them to do, and will help them to carry out his instructions in an ordered environment. He is there to teach them, not to watch them pretending to teach themselves.

This pretentious notion that classrooms containing forty children can be organised so that each child is working at his own project at his own pace is in my view a dangerous illusion, and is not only responsible for the decline in standards but also has contributed to a deterioration in child behaviour. The modern tendency to disregard the value of discipline has had grave effects on children's ability to concentrate and work hard at given tasks, and those children who grow up unacquainted with hard work never experience the excitement and sense of excellence which only achievement can bring. No one, adult or child, can work satisfactorily in the 'jolly, noisy hubbub of individual activity' so favourably described and recommended by progressive educationists, and many children today are bewildered by the rowdiness of their classrooms, which are not the havens of quiet learning which they anticipated before coming to school.

In the Ministry of Education's publication, *Primary Education*, it is admitted that progressive methods have certain disadvantages, in that some children have difficulty in concentrating under the din of activity methods. This is what it says: 'Children who have good conditions for reading at home sometimes find reading at school difficult because of the distraction of other things going on in the classroom. For their sake and even more for the sake of those who do not know quiet at home and may never achieve concentration there, teachers need to contrive times and places so that children can read at length and *in peace* [my italics]. Now that silence is no longer expected in the classroom, children's indifference to noise may be exaggerated.' What an admission!

It is the bewilderment at the noise and disorder in some schools, which makes so many little children, particularly boys, slow to learn. It is indeed significant that since the widespread adoption of activity methods in infant and junior schools there has been a noticeable difference in the measurable intellectual abilities of girls and boys. Moray House of Edinburgh, which sets Verbal Reasoning Tests for many local authorities, first noticed the superiority of girls during the war, when it was attributed to the slackening of discipline which occurred at that time. However, this superiority still exists, and has been found to be between two and four points of score, which is quite substantial. It means that allowance has to be made for it when children are being allocated to secondary schools on the results of verbal reasoning tests. Moray House, in fact, recommends that the sexes be considered independently of each other in using these tests to allot children grammar school places. The girls at eleven are superior to boys, and in my view this is the result of activity methods in the infant and junior schools. Boys are naughtier than girls, and are much less responsive to the gentle cajolery of the learning-by-stealth method. They need firm didactic teaching and despise the blandishments of those who try to jolly them into learning. They want to be told, not enticed, and many of them regard the activity and experience ruse with utter contempt. These are the ones who swell the ranks of juvenile delinquency. It is not without significance that nine out of ten juvenile offenders are boys.

As long ago as 1955, a book was published in America called *The Blackboard Jungle*, which told in novel form a terrifyingly brutal story of life in a New York slum school. The author, Evan Hunter, had experienced the shocking disciplinary conditions which he described, and he showed how the carefree modern activity theory of education bore no relation to the practicalities of the classroom. The young hoodlums depicted in this book were no doubt partly the result of their poor home environment, but also certainly they were the products of a primary school system which was based on the theories of Dewey's child-centred educational philosophy. They had always been cajoled into learning, never coerced, and they had grown up with a hearty disrespect for teachers who were afraid to lead them.

Some evidence that discipline is slipping in British schools was given at the annual conference of the Assistant Masters' Association in December 1969, where it was reported by the general secretary that after an increase in disciplinary difficulties had been noted in London schools a survey had been carried out on the subject. A total of 149 schools reported that they were experiencing serious disciplinary problems. Nearly half of this number were comprehensive, forty-six were secondary modern and twenty-one were grammar schools, and they amounted to three in ten of the schools concerned in the survey. Disciplinary offences recorded, included disturbance of lessons, absence, failure to do homework, poor standards of dress, challenges to authority, violence to staff and violence among pupils.

In January 1970 a report on discipline problems in

secondary schools was issued by the London Joint Four. The sub-committee which produced this report was composed of both headteachers and assistants, and the following is their statement of the basic problem as it affects London schools: 'There is a growing concern amongst teachers about the standards of discipline and work in secondary schools. Even where little would appear to be wrong to the casual visitor, there is evidence that a situation is developing which militates against good teaching. This is due to a slow but certain deterioration in general discipline, which can take the form of chronic class-room misbehaviour, breaches of school rules, challenges to teachers' authority (sometimes amounting to open defiance), disturbance of lessons causing much wastage of time and impeding other children from learning, litter, careless work, failure to complete work set, lateness, truancy, damage to school books and equipment, pilfering, etc., etc.

'This behaviour, which is partly due to an increase in the number of disturbed children, shows a tendency to spread. (The raising of the school leaving age may increase this tendency.)

'Causes of more serious vandalism, or of violence towards staff or fellow pupils, occur, but it is the constant disturbance caused by multiplied instances of comparatively minor misbehaviour that is becoming increasingly serious. Hours of valuable teaching time are being wasted. This fact together with the cost of repairing and replacing damaged books and property, must cause concern.

'We are most concerned for all those children who want to work and learn, but who are, for much of the time, frustrated by the troublesome minority. Furthermore, the strain on teachers is becoming increasingly severe. The temptation is to seek another post in the educational world where the problem is not so acute. In some cases, teachers have suffered nervous breakdowns, or have left the profession altogether.'

Having stated the problem in this stark and alarming manner, the report suggests that the rapid turnover in teachers produces instability in the schools and that a high proportion of young and inexperienced teachers needs much more instruction in basic classroom control. It also states that while it is obvious that the secondary schools depend on the products of the primary schools, 'it needs to be established whether the modern methods being applied in some primary schools ameliorate, or exacerbate, behaviour problems'. This statement, by implication, seems to cast some doubt on the modern child-centred theory of education, because the grave admissions of secondary school indiscipline are certainly concurrent with the adoption of the more permissive methods in the contributory infant and junior schools.

While I am sure there are no schools in this country as bad as the one in New York described by Evan Hunter, there are some which have their difficulties. I heard of such a one recently from a young teaching student who had spent her final teaching practice in a junior school where learning largely through modern informal methods, was the normal daily procedure. She had taken the top year, and found these uninhibited children very difficult to control. Strive as she did to provide interesting and exciting situations for the children to work from, she found them bored, uninterested and openly rebellious. One day a particularly difficult boy of eleven poked her in the chest with a pencil and remarked, 'Ah! Playtex Living Bra I see!' This sally was accompanied by hoots of laughter from his classmates, who were used to playing-up to their class comedian. She was so depressed at the situation in this school that she contemplated giving up teaching, but bravely stuck to her task in the hope of receiving some help from her college tutor, who made periodic visits to this junior blackboard jungle. He was not much help, however. On one occasion he sat and watched the student taking a lesson, and although the difficulties of class control were obvious, he did not intervene. After watching for ten minutes he made for the exit and tried to slip out quietly, but he left the door slightly ajar and a shouted, 'Shut the bloody door!' followed him. To his everlasting shame he came back and closed it, but did not at any time discuss the matter with the student, nor suggest ways of ameliorating her very difficult position.

There is no doubt that where, as in this case, neither the head nor the teachers have a sufficient grasp of child-centred methods to make them work satisfactorily, something approaching anarchy ensues. Such teachers and heads would be better using the old traditional formula of 'chalk and talk'.

I have indeed grave doubts about the efficacy of teaching by activity and experience, and believe that the misapplication of badly understood progressive teaching theories has caused a decline in child behaviour in many schools. I believe too that many parents and teachers have begun to have doubts about those theories. To quote Sir Cyril Burt again, 'Parents and members of the public at large, are beginning to wonder whether the free discipline, or lack of discipline, in the new permissive school may not be largely responsible for much of the subsequent delinquency, violence and general unrest that characterize our permissive society.'

While of course it would not be fair to lay on the schools all the blame for deteriorating disciplinary standards in the country at large, teachers nevertheless do have an obligation to see that as far as possible their pupils are trained to be responsible, law-abiding citizens. This training should begin from the start of school life when children are most impressionable, because lack of firm guidance in the early stages can never subsequently be repaired. This is why it is so necessary to assess if the child-centred theory of John Dewey is as effective as the traditional didactic method was in laying the early foundations of responsible child behaviour. 'As the twig is bent, so is the tree inclined!'

15

SUGGESTIONS FOR PUTTING IT RIGHT

'A child will learn—and contrary to the Rousseau school, he has to learn—to be good by being surrounded by people who are good and who expect goodness in return; he will learn to develop his intelligence by being surrounded by people who are intelligent and who keep him up to the mark.'

In this statement by John Wales in his book, *Schools of Democracy*, are implied the main objectives which I believe most parents wish to find in their children's schooling. They want them, not only to learn to be good, but to learn also to develop their intelligence to the full by contact with teachers who themselves are good and intelligent. They want, moreover, those teachers to keep the children up to the mark.

It would not have been necessary to make such a statement as this forty years ago, because at that time the standards expected of children in school were clearly defined, and teachers knew exactly where the mark was at which they must try to point their children. This, however, is not the case today. In the previous pages I have tried to show that since the abandonment of stipulated standards of achievement for the various ages of school life there has been no clear aim for the teacher to follow, and a lowered level of attainment was therefore inevitable. If children are to be left to read only when they are ready and to learn only when they want to, then who can wonder that standards fall?

It would, I am sure, not be politic or desirable to urge a return to the rigid formality of the elementary system when teachers worked to detailed schemes of work, and submitted to periodic tests of their efficiency in the classroom. However, if reasonable standards of attainment are to be achieved in the basic subjects of the curriculum, then something must be done to make the educational system more uniform than it is at present. Teachers are rightly proud of their independence in the classroom, but they must surely see that with this independence goes a responsibility to ensure that standards are maintained and if possible improved.

There is a particular need for more uniformity in the teaching of reading. I have mentioned earlier that there are in existence about forty different schemes of teaching reading, based on a variety of fundamental methods, and in these days of greater mobility of population this diversity of reading approach can be very confusing for children who remove to other schools. A child nurtured on I.T.A., for example, must find removal to a school where traditional orthography is practised very frustrating, particularly as it is likely that in the new school there will be no teacher competent to continue with I.T.A. Similar difficulties arise in transferring from a purely 'look and say' to a purely 'phonic' method. The Plowden Report, while aware of the diversity of methods in the teaching of reading, does not recommend any move to uniformity. It claims that the best teachers refuse to commit themselves to any one way, and that children 'are encouraged to try all the methods available to them and not to depend on only one method'. This does not sound very convincing to a parent who sees his child's bewilderment at what can only be regarded as a hotch-potch of reading methods. He thinks that a professional body like teachers should be able to decide which of the many reading approaches is best, and then for all schools to stick to that. This surely is where the Schools Council should come in. This organisation was set up as a central body in 1964, partly to evaluate and co-ordinate the many changes in method and curriculum which are taking place in different schools all over the country. It would appear that on this question of the many reading methods it could, by sponsoring some careful research, recommend that one of them was the most useful for the majority of British schools. After an authoritative verdict from a national body on which practising teachers are in the majority, it would not be unreasonable to ask schools to try this particular method out for a period of, say, five years. Only the most confirmed individualist could object to this mild attempt to bring some order into the present chaotic character of school reading, for I am sure that a uniformity of approach would bring a most welcome sense of methodical purpose to both teachers and children.

Teachers who think that any suggestion of keeping to a uniformity of method is an interference with their professional independence, should take comfort from the fact that doctors are content to accept the ruling of the B.M.A. on many aspects of their work, including recommendation of appropriate drugs. Reading is the most important of the basic skills in school. Surely, like doctors, teachers ought to be able to agree on what is the most efficient way of teaching this skill, and then establish a common practice which would be generally acceptable.

The teaching of English in this country is not, like reading, bedevilled by a multitude of methods. There is really no method at all. 'Just let the children write,' we are told, and apparently spelling, punctuation and syntax will look after themselves. Plowden is much in favour of 'free, fluent and copious writing', but it sadly admits, 'It is not easy to determine whether this flowering of children's writing has been accompanied by a decline in formal excellence—neatness, good handwriting, accuracy and arrangement. Some of our witnesses think it has, but few collections exist which would make possible any comparison between the writing of the thirties and that of the present day.' My own opinion, based on first-hand experience of the thirties, is that children's writing today is inferior in legibility, spelling, grammatical accuracy and quality of sentence-construction, and surely it would be surprising if this were otherwise, seeing that for the past three or four decades teachers have been enjoined not to bother about any of these fundamentals of written communication. I am dismayed but not surprised when I find such misspellings as 'daisys', 'conected', 'diference', 'begining', 'hym', 'squirrell', 'practise' for 'practice', and 'finnish' for 'finish' in the record book of a young three-year trained woman teacher. I am, moreover, not surprised that this same teacher does not understand the use of the apostrophe s, and writes 'The Heroe's'—Charles Kingsley and 'The Camels Hump'—Rudyard Kipling. It would be strange if she did not spell badly, write ungrammatically and be ignorant of the conventions of punctuation, because the whole of her education has been in the 'writing without restraint' era. Ideas for her have been more important than the style of writing them down, so how can I blame her for being what Professor Cox calls 'semi-literate'?

Caldwell Cook, author of *The Play Way*, was one of

the early advocates of uninhibited, grammar-free, creative writing. In this book, published in 1922, he said, 'Why labour to study the usual form of speech through lessons in grammar, syntax and sentence analysis when they can be safely left to look after themselves and to set the mind free to seek higher forms of self-expression?' I wonder what Cook would have thought of these lines quoted in the Plowden Report from a girl who was describing her home.

> *The smell of fish and chips*
> *Cooking in the kitchen.*
> *The baby crying for its feed*
> *And our old Dad reading the newspaper.*
> *Slippers lying around the house,*
> *And big sister telling us off.*

Would he have considered these trite phrases, written in pseudo-poetic form, to be one of the higher forms of self-expression?

Is it not time we had a reappraisal of the 'non-method' of teaching English in our schools, and ask ourselves if Caldwell Cook's advice to leave grammar, syntax and sentence-construction to look after themselves has been sound? When students at colleges of education have to be taught to spell correctly and write grammatically, then it is time to drop that pretentious term 'creative writing' and get back to the teaching of the basic fundamentals which will ensure that most children leave school able to write their mother tongue in a conventionally acceptable form. This will mean a return to spelling lists and dictation in all classes of the junior school and the earlier forms of the secondaries. It will mean, too, that correct punctuation and grammatical construction must be insisted upon in all forms of writing, and that some formal lessons on the correction of common faults will have to be taken, as was the general practice until the craze for free expression swept into our schools. When children have mastered the basic fundamentals of written English and have begun to take pride in accurately written language, they will find, surprisingly, that ideas will flow more freely than before, because they will now have the skill to set their thoughts down in a form which others can take a pleasure in reading. They will discover, like Coleridge, that 'Putting the right words in the right order' is the basis of all successful writing.

The third 'R', arithmetic, has been replaced by Mathematics in our schools, and while some revision of the traditional 'ten sums a day' method of teaching was perhaps inevitable, we must not overlook the need for a thorough and systematic approach to this important subject. Children in the infant and junior departments will still have to be grounded in the hard facts of number, and the four rules in arithmetic must still be the basis of the work there. While intelligent children can be introduced at an earlier age than formerly to a number of interesting modern mathematical topics, it is useless to pretend that the less-gifted can do the same kind of work. Dabbling in fanciful non-essentials is a waste of time for these children. They need systematic training in calculation and manipulation of number before proceeding to theoretical work which is not firmly based on the concrete quantities which they are capable of understanding. In the case of mathematics, as in reading, it should be possible through the Schools Council to decide on a generally acceptable outline of work for different age-groups, and on reasonable standards of achievement at various levels of schooling.

Certainly something must be done to ensure that there are some common aims and standards of attainment in the three basic subjects of the school curriculum, and that teachers in all parts of the country are aware of those aims. The secondary schools have their standards set by the General Certificate and the Certificate of Secondary Education, and a way must be found of providing the primary schools with a similar objective. The Schools Council should be able to provide suggestions for common standards in junior schools, and after consultation with the teachers' professional organisations and their approval, these could be used as a basis for work in the classroom. It is important that those schools which have adopted such modern progressive approaches to learning as are contained in the 'integrated day' and 'centre of interest' methods, shall have some stipulated standards for guidelines. Where teachers believe that 'inherent motivation' is preferable to the 'imposed' kind, they will surely not object that parents of children in their schools expect standards comparable to those in formal traditional schools where a set time-table and syllabuses are in operation. There is no need for a dictated uniformity of method if a sensible safeguarding of standards is maintained.

Having said something about the desirability of a mark or level of attainment for the three basic subjects of the curriculum, it is necessary to consider the people who are trained to keep the children 'up to the mark'. In our haste to expand the education service and lengthen the period of compulsory attendance at school we have created a need for more and more teachers, but we have rarely had, until recently, enough teachers to meet this need. Reduction in the size of classes and the raising of the leaving age to sixteen in 1972 will further stretch the capacity of the training colleges, and there will indoubtedly be more teaching vacancies than personnel to fill them. This is in my view a bad policy. The quality of the teachers is more important than their number as any headteacher knows. A good teacher will have a better effect on fifty children than two indifferent teachers taking two classes of twenty-five. I think we have too many indifferent teachers and far too big a turnover of staffs, particularly in primary schools. Over half the women teachers today are married, and the wastage as these become mothers is very high. As Plowden says, 'The exodus has been catastrophic; the return slow.'

Frequent changes of staff have the worst possible effect on a school, particularly today, when methods and standards are not uniform throughout the country. Children need above all things stability of background for sound development, and in many schools undue turnover of staff prevents this. I mentioned earlier that I thought five 'O' levels taken in a single-subject examination were not sufficient to ensure that we have good-quality teachers, and I am sure that further hurried expansion of the educational service can only further reduce that quality. More has certainly meant worse in the case of teachers, because as the number of personnel increases, the cost of the educational service rises, and successive governments have been reluctant to increase salaries on account of the enormous cost to the economy. Moreover, as teachers' salaries have lagged behind those of people in other comparable jobs, teaching becomes less and less attractive to good-quality men and women. It would be advantageous for the educational service and the country if it had fewer but better-qualified and better-paid teachers, than to expand as it has done at the cost of quality. We ought to take a leaf out of the doctors' book and restrict entry to the teaching profession to people of high calibre. We should then be esteemed more highly and could command better remuneration for a most exacting job.

Having improved the standards of entrance to the profession, something must be done to ensure that all students are trained in the practical side of teaching. They must first of all be given systematic instruction in the methods appertaining to the various subjects they are going to teach. Prospective infant and junior teachers must know in detail all about the many reading schemes and understand the numerous aids to the teaching of number and mathematics. They must also be made aware of the duties they will be called on to carry out in the classroom and school. Above all, they must be shown by expert exponents of the teaching craft how to create a classroom atmosphere where children will wish to work to their fullest capacity. As practical training like this can only be carried out satisfactorily by successful classroom practitioners, some method of exchange between college lecturers and the best teachers in the schools would seem to be the solution. Students would then have the benefit of training by competent teachers, and the lecturers would surely profit by refresher periods in the schools.

Whether college lecturers would agree to this secondment to the classroom is questionable, but the improvement in teacher training resulting from such an arrangement would be beneficial to the schools. To return to the quotation by John Wales, at the beginning, if we want our children to learn to be good and intelligent we must insist that the colleges of education provide the schools with the good and intelligent people who are capable of keeping our Tommies well up to the mark.

POSTSCRIPT

Because the standards of written expression in English have fallen so much in recent years, certain universities have requested that students seeking admission should take a Use of English examination paper in addition to their Advanced Levels. The comments shown below are taken verbatim from the Report of Examiners in July 1969 on the Use of English paper set by one of the boards.

'The general standard of work was very disappointing, though there were some able candidates. Others, however, submitted the poorest answers yet seen in this series of examinations.

'An occupational hazard of marking is that some answers are difficult to read. The paper under scrutiny, however, produced many more than usual. The difficulty of deciphering ill-written italic has been complained of before; this time there were many scripts penned in a microscopically small hand or in letters that were large and ill formed. The few candidates who favour felt-tipped pens should pass these without delay to their greengrocers. What cannot be read, or can be read only slowly or with difficulty, militates against itself. A few candidates, on the other hand, handed in work that was neat and contained few errors of spelling and grammar but was nevertheless incomprehensible: instances of this kind have been quoted previously. Some work had to be studied with the attention of a press-reader looking for literals.

'Some candidates were ill-prepared (in essay-writing, especially, they had had little practice), but read over their work before handing it in: solecisms like 'are' for 'and' were common. The candidate who uses the apostrophe correctly and who encloses within quotation-marks the words he cites from the paper and from elsewhere is becoming rarer and rarer, and miscopyings from the question paper itself are increasing. It is not always the long or difficult word that is misspelt; indeed, prominent in the list of spelling errors were cognates of the word 'occur'.

'It is, then, in their expression rather than in their understanding (though this is far from perfect) of English that many candidates do not do themselves justice.'